MARYADA

Praise for *Maryada*

'This wise commentary that deeply enhances our understanding of the Ramayana should be an essential read for our times that insist on a monochromatic interpretation of the epic.'

– ASHUTOSH BHARDWAJ, *The Hindustan Times*

'An excellent read ... engaging and reader-friendly, without losing academic rigour.'

– BIBEK DEBROY, *Open*

'Offer[s] unique and distinctive insights. It is also characterized by a deep-rooted affection and compassion for the people in the epic. [Sattar] has an ability to see and understand them not just as characters, but as living and breathing beings negotiating through the complex, thorny issues of being human.'

– SAMHITA ARNI, *Mumbai Mirror*

'In her erudite yet conversational style, Sattar unpeels the layers of uncertainty that elude the public's simplistic understanding of the epic's moral arc as one where good triumphs over evil.'

– SOMAK GHOSHAL, *Mint Lounge*

MARYADA

SEARCHING FOR DHARMA IN THE RAMAYANA

ARSHIA SATTAR

HarperCollins *Publishers* India

First published in hardback in India in 2020 by
HarperCollins *Publishers*
4th Floor, Tower A, Building No. 10, DLF Cyber City,
DLF Phase II, Gurugram, Haryana – 122002
www.harpercollins.co.in

This edition published in India by HarperCollins *Publishers* 2023

2 4 6 8 10 9 7 5 3 1

P-ISBN: 978-93-5699-429-4
E-ISBN: 978-93-5357-713-1

Typeset in 11.5/15 Arno Pro at
Manipal Digital Systems, Manipal

Printed and bound at
Nutech Print Services - India

FSC
www.fsc.org
MIX
Paper from responsible sources
FSC® C143748

This book is printed on FSC® certified paper
which ensures responsible forest management.

Then came the Treta Yuga, where the men of glory were kshatriyas, and they ruled as the brahmins had done before ... Brahmins had been superior to the kshatriyas, but in this yuga, both were equal in power.

– Valmiki's Ramayana (Uttara Kanda 65.11–12)

Now hear from me about the Treta Yuga in which sacrifice flourishes and dharma is reduced by one quarter ... People stand in their own dharma and act in accordance with it.

– The Mahabharata (Vana Parvan 148.22–25)

CONTENTS

INTRODUCTION

While we are accustomed to acknowledging that the Mahabharata does not provide us with either a consistent or a coherent idea of what dharma is, we look to the Ramayana with great hope to resolve the most fundamental of human questions: What does it mean to be good? The Mahabharata tells us over and over again that dharma is 'sukshma' – subtle, elusive, hard to know. It is a refrain, almost, in this rich and complex Sanskrit text of one hundred thousand verses, attributed to Vyasa but composed over centuries, which folds within itself many and different ideas of dharma. The Ramayana, however, composed alongside the Mahabharata over the same centuries and in the same political and social milieu, subject to the same influences and tensions, never tells us that dharma is beyond the reach of human understanding, and therefore, of human action. On the contrary, each of the Ramayana's principal characters believes that it is possible, and that it is necessary that they act on the basis of this slippery code which governs each and every aspect of an individual's life.[1]

Rather than provide a conclusive definition of dharma in the Ramayana, the essays in this book seek the various boundaries that different ideas of dharma come up against, boundaries beyond which actions become transgressive and deserving of punishment. 'Maryada' is a commonly used word for 'boundary' in Sanskrit. It also means 'propriety of conduct', and with this additional connotation, it holds within itself the idea that the boundary it refers to cannot be crossed without some kind of retributive action. In the context of the Ramayana tradition, the word maryada carries a special weight precisely because the word comes to be used as Rama's defining virtue. Within the tradition, and especially after the later Ramayanas, Rama becomes known as the 'maryada purushottama', the ideal man. In fact, it could well be that the meaning of 'maryada' as 'good conduct' comes from Rama's essential association with the concept of propriety itself.[2]

Despite the fact that the Ramayana's hero, Rama, is regarded as the epitome of dharma in his thoughts and deeds, the Ramayana cannot provide us with a single template for right action.[3] Unlike the Mahabharata, the Ramayana shows us,

---

1 Valmiki's Ramayana, the earliest of the canonized Rama stories, does not intend to be a manual of ethics. However, as Rama developed into a culture's ideal man, his actions and behaviour became increasingly paradigmatic, and so, we must examine the ethical foundations that the Valmiki Ramayana presents, however unintended they may be.

2 This idea is discussed at greater length later in the Introduction.

3 The Mahabharata, on the other hand, has long 'samvada' sections where the principles of dharma are elucidated, often through discursive

with compassion and tenderness, that whoever we are, dharma is always and everywhere about a multiplicity of appropriate choices, that when we choose one way of being and doing over another, we will as often be wrong as we are right. When Rama tells his mother Kaushalya that he will obey his father's wish and go into the forest for fourteen years, her anguished question to him is why he privileges his duty as a son to his father over his obligations to her as a mother. When Vibhishana decides to do what he believes to be right, his alliance with Rama is predicated on the betrayal which leads to the killing of his brother. When Kaikeyi deprives Rama of his right to be king, she acts for the benefit of her son and legitimately asks for the redemption of boons she was given as well as for the fulfilment of a promise made to her father. But she humiliates her husband and makes a mockery of Kosala's widely held reputation as a kingdom of righteousness. The actors in the Ramayana can see all the choices before them; their problem is not that dharma is sukshma, it is that dharma presents the individual with more than one equal and legitimate choice.

In her book *The Origins of Evil in Hindu Mythology* (Berkeley: University of California Press, 1976), Wendy Doniger brings to our notice the fact that, until the bhakti period, there are multiple dharmas that impinge upon an individual's conscience as the possible bases of action. There is the dharma of the self, svadharma, determined by who one is; there is varnashrama dharma depending on one's caste and station in life; there is

---

conversation, and sometimes, through stories. The Valmiki Ramayana also has discussions on dharma, but they are neither that long nor that systematized in terms of what to do in what kind of situation.

samanya dharma, or general principles that apply to everyone; and there is, over and above all of these, sanatana dharma which is eternal, and one imagines, immutable. Each additional articulation of dharma represents an increasingly complex ontology in the development of Hinduism. As schools of Hindu thought explore their understanding of the individual self in relation to perceived and ultimate realities, their ideas of what underpins individual ethics and moral action, too, become more expansive. Ancient rituals and social segregation are maintained as the self is placed in an increasingly interconnected world, and theories of action begin to respond to more sophisticated metaphysics and theologies.

Given the many regulatory principles that developed over the centuries to inform early Hindu belief and practice, the magnificent epic narratives which present us with an entire spectrum of human (and divine) possibility became the repositories where these ideas of the right and the good were juxtaposed against each other and explored to their fullest. Composed and redacted as it was over nearly a millennium, a text like the Valmiki Ramayana seems to have absorbed all these various ontological and ethical hypotheses as well as their contradictions. The Sanskrit Ramayana's earliest roots lie in the period just after the Vedas and their associated texts (the Brahmanas and the Aranyakas). Its story blossomed during the centuries when the Upanishads, Jainism and Buddhism turned the search for individual liberation away from worldly activities and towards internal contemplation. They reflected the decline of a religiously monopolistic priestly class, and the rise of a ruling elite of warriors and kings who also laid claim to spiritual knowledge. They also told stories of the power of renunciation and valorized the ascetic life over attachment to sensory pleasures of the world which were, in some schools of thought, fleeting and illusory.

The conflicting values of the philosopher seeking a personal truth beyond perceived reality and the king who needs to maintain social and political order in the mundane world come together in both the epics, but are more clearly visible in the relatively simpler, basically linear narrative of the Ramayana. As the Valmiki text continued to grow, it picked up elements from the discourses, both theological as well as those related to caste and dharma, that surrounded it. Ideas from the Dharma Shastras and the early Mahapuranas slipped into the text, transforming the nature (and quite possibly the intent) of its earliest narrative layers. By the time of Kamban's twelfth-century *Iramavataram* in Tamil, bhakti had drenched the story of Rama, making it, for all practical purposes, a redemptive tale of god acting on earth to vanquish evil and to reward his devotees.

On the most basic level, within the Hindu system, a person is both an individual self and a representative member of their caste. Thus, in terms of choosing a basis for action, they might consider svadharma, which would be unique and subjective and a matter of their choice as an individual, or varnashrama dharma, which would be dictated by their caste and stage in life. The Bhagavad Gita movingly explores Arjuna's debilitating existential moment framed in exactly these terms. As a kshatriya, the war against his cousins, an event that he has trained for all his life, should be the crowning moment of his glorious career as a warrior. But as an individual, he finds himself unable to raise arms and prepare to kill members of his family, his elders and his teachers. Even Krishna is not able to resolve this dilemma in favour of one or the other dharma, and so, he offers the troubled warrior the best of both worlds. He tells Arjuna that, as a kshatriya, it is his duty to fight to the fullest, but as an individual, he can surrender himself to Krishna and allow god to carry the burden of his actions. Arjuna can now perform the actions that he must as a warrior, but as a singular human being he can be liberated from his attachment to their consequences. What Arjuna has not taken into account in his moment of crisis is samanya dharma, or the code of conduct that applies to all people, which would include such injunctions as ahimsa – 'do not cause harm/injury'. More accurately perhaps, he has decided that the duties arising from his varna (caste) dharma as a kshatriya are more important at this moment than a generalized commitment to ahimsa.

The rise of various heterodox traditions (such as Jainism and Buddhism) around the sixth and fifth centuries BCE, with their rejection of caste hierarchies and blood sacrifices, and with their emphasis on an unmediated path to spiritual truth, provided a constellation of new ideas that orthodox Hinduism had to contend with. It is likely that samanya dharma, suggesting some general rules of conduct that applied to all human beings, developed as a way of incorporating egalitarian principles that mitigated the differences of varna dharma into religious and social practice. In the same period, within the so-called orthodox traditions (that accept the ultimate authority of the Vedas), the consolidation of Upanishadic thought via Badarayana's Brahma Sutras, for example, offered an alternative understanding of the 'truth' and of the individual soul's relationship both with the world and with the ultimate reality. Samanya dharma was likely to have been elevated to the idea of sanatana dharma, eternal dharma, in order to resonate more fully with the philosophy of the Vedanta school.

The Valmiki Ramayana proved responsive to these changes in the social, religious and aesthetic environment, enriching its narrative about an exiled prince and his abducted wife by exploring the various ethical dilemmas that a man could face, dilemmas that bear upon both his private and his public self. As much as the Mahabharata is a story about how to deal with those from whom one has become estranged, the Ramayana is a story about how to act well with those with whom one is most intimate. Rama's crises are all related to the people he loves best – his parents, his wife, his brothers – and though he appears not to falter in these life-altering moments, his frequent conversations with Lakshmana about dharma and the hierarchy of values in which it is placed show us that the text itself is negotiating the path to goodness.

The Hindu epics are not only interested in the establishment of dharma, they are also compelled to examine the places and situations in which dharma breaks down or is disputed or contentious. As a genre text, the Ramayana conforms to the literary tropes and narrative strategies of other epics and locates the challenges to dharma as a code of how to be in the larger world – in places outside the city, in forests and in the wilderness. These are the places where the human princes encounter behaviours they have never seen before and cannot understand. Everything seems to be opposed to what they have known from the city. In the forest, women make sexual advances towards men but they also live as ascetics, brother kills brother over a disputed throne, and rakshasas can live by codes that endorse violence and avarice. Each of these dharmas throws the practices of Ayodhya into relief. It is outside the familiar spaces of Ayodhya (where patterns of behaviour are more or less predictable and dharma is protected by the righteous kings of the Ikshvaku dynasty) that Rama acts in the most unexpected ways – he urges Lakshmana to mutilate Shurpanakha and he kills Vali who is fighting another opponent. Rama and Lakshmana are sure that the sanctioned behaviour of the beings who live outside the city constitutes 'adharma' – which should mean either the oppositional anti-dharma or the lack of dharma, rather than a different idea of dharma altogether – and they act swiftly to punish the transgressors.

It is as if the city is the boundary within which societies can flourish in their unique coherence and with a single dharma in operation. While cities can only accommodate one dharma at a time, the forest (or rather, any space outside the city) is an indeterminate space where multiple dharmas can coexist. It is a space of fluidity, where shapes can change and where unusual and challenging choices become available. Many scholars have pointed to the fact that, in literatures across the world, spaces outside the city are seen as liminal zones, spaces where transgressions can occur without retribution. The rules of the city do not apply, characters come up against the unexpected, the magical and the dangerous. Accentuating the difference between the forest and the city is the fact that, when transgressive behaviours or acts (which might have been 'allowed' in the forests and in the wilderness) are committed within the city, they lead to disaster. A determined way of life is threatened, and quite often, shaken. Transgressive behaviours have to be contained or uprooted for order to be maintained in the city.

In the case of the Ramayana, these transgressions within the city are catastrophic. Dasharatha's surrender to Kaikeyi's demands goes against the dharma that prevails in Ayodhya, where, apart from the established tradition of primogeniture, the norms of behaviour are about restraint and the public good. For Rama and Sita, it is the return to Ayodhya and its stringent dharma with regard to women's behaviour that leads to the tragedy that lies at the heart of the Ramayana, that of Rama and Sita's final separation. Once he is back in Ayodhya, with its restrictive moralities and codes of conduct, Rama assumes the role of a king and banishes his pregnant wife into the forest because his people question her chastity. It is as if the agnipariksha, the trial by fire, that proved Sita's innocence on the battlefield in front of the monkeys and the rakshasas is not sufficient proof for Ayodhya. In places where dharmas other than the human dharma upheld by Ayodhya prevailed, Sita could be considered chaste after the agnipariksha that she asked for to prove her innocence. But Ayodhya cannot accept this proof of the trial by fire, even though it was a trial blessed by the gods. It appears that Ayodhya cannot even countenance the possibility that an abducted woman might have remained unmolested. Rama sacrifices his personal happiness for the sake of Ayodhya's dharma, sending his beloved wife away from the city that will not take her back into its fold. When Sita does return, summoned by Valmiki to Rama's great sacrifice where the story of his life is being recited, Rama has already been reunited with his sons. Asked to prove her chastity once more in the presence of Ayodhya's citizens, this time, it is Sita who goes away, rejecting both her husband and the city that has bound him within its moral strictures. Sita leaves Rama, Ayodhya and her sons behind as she disappears into the earth, never to return. Her presence in Ayodhya has become irrelevant, for with Rama's sons having been publicly pronounced legitimate by Valmiki at the sacrifice, Ayodhya's future is secure.

But it is also in the dangerous forest that Rama is exposed to the quiet, contemplative lives of the ascetic communities. Their way of life encourages him to examine the dharma that he was born into, a dharma that he sees as essentially predicated on violence, however justifiable that violence may be. Rama thinks about all that has happened to him, based as it is on the dharma of kshatriyas as understood and practised by his father and stepmother. He begins to consider the more abstract and immutable principles that could guide a man's life and reaches for an eternal dharma that transcends the ethics of person, place and time. Like Yudhishthira in the Mahabharata, who was also profoundly influenced by his conversations with sages during his forest exile, Rama becomes attracted to the idea that a king should be righteous as well as rightful. More and more, Rama seeks a righteousness not based in caste or life-stage, but in a higher truth which an individual can grasp through intuition. As kshatriyas who seek such a truth, Rama and Yudhishthira resemble the wise kings in the Upanishads (such as Ajatashatru and Janaka), but in their reluctance to accept the kingship that is rightfully theirs, they point to the lives and choices of the historical Buddha and Mahavira, both princes who renounced the world.

However, even within Ayodhya, dharma is not uncontested. Lakshmana challenges Rama's idea of what is right when he prepares to obey the wishes of his father and go into exile. Lakshmana believes that the old king should be imprisoned because, of course, he is acting against the laws of Ayodhya, but more importantly, because he is being unjust to his heir and to his people. Bharata, too, decides to act against his father's wishes and his mother's ambitions as he tries his best to persuade Rama to give up his exile and reclaim the throne. Ultimately, Bharata rules in Rama's name for fourteen years, thus both upholding and flouting Dasharatha's decree. In Dasharatha's time, Ayodhya's court is guided by Vasishtha, the gentle family priest, but he too faces opposition from the brahmin Jabali who assures Rama that he is under no obligation to respect his father's wishes since an individual's first duty is to himself.[4] Later, when Rama returns from exile, Agastya, who is more aggressively brahminical, becomes his primary adviser and Rama is persuaded that the dharma of kingship urges him in the direction of renouncing first his wife, and then, his brother.

The choices contained within a dharma determined by caste and life-stage and circumstance in the present are not the only things that create the horizon of an individual's possible actions. Hindu epics are driven by four 'operators', as it were: dharma, karma, vidhi (fate) and daiva (intervention

[4] The fact that, in some versions of Valmiki's text, Jabali recants his arguments against the dharma of family obligations supports the hypothesis that the Sanskrit Ramayana is acknowledging the multiple theories of ontology and ethics that prevailed at the time of its composition.

by the gods).[5] Dharma and karma are intrinsic to an individual character's actions, that is, how those actions are determined by a character's past deeds and how those characters choose to act given the choices before them in the present. Take Dasharatha, for example. His dharma as a husband requires that he honour the boons he gave his wife many years before, but his karma for having inadvertently killed a young ascetic ensures that he, too, will suffer a heart-wrenching separation from his beloved child. Both his karma and his dharma coincide such that he is compelled by his own deeds to send his beloved Rama into exile.

Vidhi and daiva are what act upon a character from outside and they, too, determine the course of the narrative and what happens to a character. Unwilling to hold his father responsible for what he has done, Rama casts about for reasons that could explain this unexpected change in his circumstances. As a counterpoint to the moral choices that dharma implies, Rama suggests to Lakshmana that it can only be fate that has brought him to this life crisis, that Kaikeyi was but an instrument of a larger force that had pushed his life in another direction, and that he was resigned to whatever lay ahead. Rama points to vidhi as the cause for what has happened to him since he has

---

5 In a classroom lecture (University of Chicago, 1986) A.K. Ramanujan pointed out that for epic characters, in general, fate and the gods propel the story and describe a character's narrative arc. (Oedipus, for example, caught in a bitter squabble between the gods Apollo and Diana, is fated to kill his father and marry his mother, which is what he does despite every attempt by his parents and himself to prevent that from happening.) But in the Hindu epics, the moral force of dharma and the retributive force of karma also drive the narrative.

done nothing in the past that could have merited this cataclysm. Lakshmana argues that surrendering to fate is the refuge of the weak, and that a brave kshatriya like Rama is bound to stand against such a fate if it leads to injustice. The gods also intervene more overtly on the side of those whom they favour: in the final battle with Ravana, Indra sends his chariot and his charioteer Matali to help Rama vanquish the mighty rakshasa even though he is already vulnerable to his human opponent. And so it is that in two critical moments of his public life – the moment of his exile and the moment of his killing Ravana – Rama is acted upon by forces that are beyond him, and are not determined by choices that he has made or by things that he has done.

The possibility of pure action led only by the principles of (any) dharma is also militated against by boons and curses in the story which are sometimes, though not always, uttered by the gods. Thus, Ravana is made exceedingly powerful by Brahma's boon of invincibility to all beings except humans, but he is constrained in his behaviour by the curse of Rambha. We have already noted how a curse from the parents of the young ascetic he had killed leads to Dasharatha's sorrow and untimely death, and changes the course of Rama's life.

With all these multiple, and sometimes contradictory, factors at work in the narrative, the path of dharma is hardly smooth, nor is it clear what is right for whom and when. Different orders of beings, such as the vanaras and the rakshasas, live by codes that often run counter to those of humans, cities tend to hold rather more rigid rules of behaviour within their walls and these become troublesome when they are applied elsewhere, forests are fluid spaces where challenges to the more conventional ways of living flourish, the quietude of ascetics and the serenity achieved by renunciants hold a dangerous attraction. The codes of conduct by which others live place Rama's own ideas about what dharma is into relief, and like him, we wonder if the dharma of city dwellers is based entirely in social roles and convention. Rama acknowledges the symbiotic relationship between dharma and karma when he says that he does not want to violate dharma because such a transgression would surely affect his future lives.

The essays in this volume attempt to make sense of the multiple values that dharma can have, and also the diverse ways in which dharmic choices can be understood and justified. Further, dharma is rooted differently for different characters in the story – in justice for Lakshmana, in truth for Rama, in one's own actions and promises for Dasharatha, in the constancy of love for Sita. As readers of the text, we are critical of many of these understandings and the choices made therefrom, but by showing us that even Rama questions dharma, the text perhaps invites us to do the same. Rama questions dharma not in order to reject it altogether, but to reach a deeper and fuller understanding of what it could mean to him as an individual, and whether that subjective understanding can be made a universal wellspring for human action.

Rama has seen many kinds of dharma played out before him, and he has heard an equal number of arguments for one way of behaving over another. His own ideas of what is good have been tested, never more so than when he does what he believes to be right, even what he knows will not be to his advantage, and when his actions result in unhappy circumstances for all concerned. Rama has been thinking about dharma, not only as a basis for moral action, but more fundamentally, about how he can be righteous with confidence and belief rather than simply by conforming to the social codes prescribed for him. We know that dharma demands that an individual choose between many paths of action that all seem appropriate – Rama seeks the foundation of dharma so that he always makes the right choice for himself. As he thinks more about this, and as he is confronted with different ways of thinking about what is right (whether it is his father's acquiescence to Kaikeyi's wishes or Vali's actions as king), Rama's articulation of the fundamental basis of righteousness becomes refined. He moves from holding that a particularized individual dharma is the only basis for choice (obviously limited) to the more radical idea that dharma *is* the truth that transcends all boundaries.[6]

Valmiki's text puts different ideas of dharma in conversation with each other, and as the hero of the story who must find resolution (for himself, if not for anyone else), it is Rama who pushes against the dharma that he is bound to uphold. As the Ramayana develops into a story about an ideal man who is also god on earth, Rama defines and is defined by the boundaries of dharma. When Rama is called 'maryada purushottama', the larger tradition tells us to understand the phrase simply as 'ideal man'. More accurately, it could be translated either as 'the best of all men who (know) the limits (of moral action)' or 'the best of men who is the limit (of moral action)'. By the latter

[6] In seeking a dharma that essentially goes beyond the particularity of an individual self (varnashrama dharma, svadharma and svabhava), Rama is, I believe, seeking a way to an ultimate truth which transcends the self entirely. In this complete coincidence of dharma and truth, we are presented with the tautology of truth is dharma, dharma is truth.

definition, dharma is what Rama does – that becomes axiomatic when we know Rama to be god. But the former explanation is more interesting, and I believe that is what the middle books of Valmiki's text explore.

In pursuing this search for a true and eternal dharma along with Rama, we are offered a chance to read the Valmiki Ramayana as a locus for a religion forming itself around a great central idea, the idea of dharma. In Valmiki's middle books, the principles of dharma are still being discussed, individual and caste dharma are still being weighed against each other, temporal power, held by warriors and kings, is testing its might against the spiritual power held by priests. The consequences of these alternative bases for action are played out in the choices that Rama makes for his own life, and in the lives of those around him. It would appear that no two characters in the Ramayana apprehend dharma in the same way. Perhaps more accurately, they do not see the choices that dharma offers them in the same way that others do.

While the Mahabharata circles around many of the same problems with dharma, it reminds us over and over again that dharma lies beyond the reach of the human imagination. At best, we can be taught the principles of dharma by those who are older and wiser. The Ramayana, on the other hand, holds out the promise that everyone can and should search for a dharma they can believe in, a dharma that is vulnerable but all the more precious because it has been sought and found rather than given and received. It may not prevent us from making mistakes, but like Rama, it will help us to live with their consequences.

DASHARATHA'S DILEMMA

If we work with the well-established assumption that the Bala Kanda is a later addition to the middle books of what we call the Valmiki Ramayana, our first encounter with Dasharatha is in the Ayodhya Kanda. We see him in his court, where he announces to all who are gathered there – his courtiers, ministers, subjects and vassal kings – that he is about to abdicate and anoint his eldest and best-beloved son, Rama, king of Kosala in his place. Dasharatha is majestic in this moment. He speaks of having discharged his duties fully and well, of having grown old under the shadow of the royal umbrella, about the appropriateness of choosing Rama as his successor. His voice is as 'deep as thunder, as resonant as a bell'.[1] He is a monarch in complete control of his kingdom and its destiny as he reminds Rama about the duties and obligations of a king. All those who hear him are moved by his dignity and joyfully accept the transition that he is suggesting.

He leaves the great hall and consults astrologers and advisers about the auspicious time for Rama's coronation. Then, Dasharatha has a moment of doubt. He summons Rama to his

---

[1] Arshia Sattar (tr.), *Valmiki's Ramayana* (New Delhi: HarperCollins India, 2019), chap. 13.

private chambers and tells him of the nightmares he has been having, filled with dire portents that bode great misfortune for himself and his kingdom. Dasharatha's own birth star is in the grip of malignant forces and he begs Rama to make sure that the coronation proceeds as planned before he, the king, changes his mind. Strangely prescient in this moment of panic, Dasharatha says that he wants to crown Rama while Bharata, his son from Kaikeyi, is still away visiting his mother's family:

> 'Rama, make sure that I anoint you before I change my mind, for the human heart cannot be trusted! ... I have a strong feeling that I should install you as my heir while your brother Bharata is away from the city. He is an honourable and righteous man, devoted to his elders and slow to anger, but I know that the human mind is fickle. However, even he will have to honour an act that has been accomplished.'[2]

The contrast between the steadfast Ikshvaku monarch in his court and the uncertain old man who cannot even be sure of his own actions could not be more stark. And yet, from this point onwards in the story, Dasharatha is more and more an insecure old man, haunted by bad dreams, fearful about the love of his family, unsure of what he must do next, caught in a dilemma that springs from deeds and promises made in his past. With the benefit of hindsight, since it is composed later, the Bala Kanda picks up on Dasharatha's weakness and his tendency to have his judgement clouded by emotion. In this book which precedes

---

2 Sattar, *Valmiki's Ramayana*, chap. 13.

the Ayodhya Kanda in the narrative, Dasharatha's weakness is presented to us as the sentimental attachment that an older father has for a much-awaited son, born late in his life and all the more beloved for being so. When Vishvamitra comes to Dasharatha and asks for Rama to fight the yakshini Tataka who has been disrupting the ascetic practice and holy rituals of the great sage, Dasharatha reacts thus:

> Dasharatha lost consciousness for a moment and when he had recovered, he said, 'My lotus-eyed Rama is only fifteen years old. I don't think he can face the rakshasas in battle! Take my entire army with me as the commander. My men are brave and heroic and skilled with their weapons. I will go with my warriors to fight the rakshasas. We are capable of facing them. But do not ask for Rama!
>
> 'With my bow and my arrows I will lead the army myself and I will fight the rakshasas until my last breath. We shall protect you and you can complete your ritual without any further obstructions. I will come with you, but do not take Rama!
>
> 'He is only a child and his education is not yet complete. He does not know strength from weakness. He does not have the required skill with weapons nor is he seasoned in battle. He cannot face the rakshasas who fight unfairly!
>
> 'I cannot bear the thought of living without Rama for even a day. Do not take him away! ... I am sixty thousand years old and I obtained my son with great difficulty. Do not take Rama away!'[3]

---

[3] Sattar, *Valmiki's Ramayana*, chap. 5.

The old king does whatever he can to protect his young son from the dangers of what is surely going to be an unequal encounter. But Vishvamitra is not to be swayed, and in the end, Rama and Lakshmana leave the palace with the sage. Of course, all goes well – Rama proves himself in the encounter with Tataka and her sons, and in return, Vishvamitra bestows upon the young princes knowledge of magical weapons that will come when they are called. Perhaps that was always Vishvamitra's intention: that the journey with him was not only to kill Tataka, but also to fortify the princes with weapons that would stand them in good stead for all that lay ahead.

If we were to start with the Ayodhya Kanda as the first book of the Ramayana, we would meet the princes as young adults. But the Bala Kanda has the opportunity to speak of the birth of Rama and his brothers – a birth which is aided by the intervention of divine forces, like that of all epic heroes.[4] Dasharatha the wise, just and beloved king of Ayodhya has a daughter but no sons. He is advised by Sumantra to persuade the young sage Rishyashringa, son of Vibhandaka, to perform the sacrifice that will lead to the birth of sons. Through a clever ruse which involves the courtesans of the city, the innocent, forest-dwelling sage is brought to Ayodhya and commences the special rituals from the Atharva Veda by which Dasharatha's queens will become pregnant. As the gods come together to gather their share of the sacrifice, they decide that Vishnu must come to earth in human form, as one of Dasharatha's sons, in

---

4 Dasharatha obliquely refers to this divine intervention in the speech quoted above when he tells Vishvamitra, in the Bala Kanda, that Rama is doubly precious because he was obtained with 'great difficulty'.

order to kill the rakshasa Ravana who is tormenting the three worlds. In a delightful coincidence of needs that only an epic can devise, Dasharatha's desire for a son on earth matches the gods' requirement for a human womb[5] into which one of them can be born, and so, Vishnu comes into the world of men as Rama Dasharathi, prince of Ayodhya. The divine and the mundane come together in Rama's person, and the different realms they represent are united when Rama lives as the human prince whose wife is abducted and as the man-god who must kill the rakshasa who threatens the worlds. In the Bala Kanda, we have encountered Dasharatha as a father rather than as a mighty monarch. This father returns in the Ayodhya Kanda when Dasharatha pleads with Rama to protect him from himself by ensuring that the coronation is not delayed because 'the human mind is fickle', indicating that circumstances might cause him to change his mind. But he is also speaking as a king who has given his word in public about his successor and, in that sense, he is asking Rama to help him keep that promise, a promise which lies in the realm of his duties as a king.

Rama goes away to tell his mother the news that he is to be crowned the very next day, and almost at the same moment, Dasharatha is summoned to the apartments of his younger wife, Kaikeyi. He enters there to find Kaikeyi in a towering rage, lying on the floor with her hair in disarray and her ornaments flung from her body.

---

5 Vishnu must come to earth as a man in order to kill Ravana who has a boon that makes him invulnerable to all creatures except humans.

> He caressed her gently with deep humility, as a tusker might stroke his mate who has been injured by a hunter's arrow.
>
> The lovelorn king spoke anxiously. 'Has someone been rude to you or spoken to you harshly? ... Could I have displeased you in any way? ... Is there anything I can do to make you happy? Would you like an innocent man punished? Or a guilty man set free? I will do anything you ask, even give up my life!'[6]

For a king who has just announced in public that he lives by dharma, this last statement is extraordinary. The law books insist that one of the most important responsibilities of a king is to punish the guilty and protect the innocent. Everything that Dasharatha has stood for vanishes in the presence of Kaikeyi, especially in the shadow of her displeasure. The scene that follows is surely one of the most heart-wrenching in the entire Ramayana. A great king is brought to his knees, literally, by the petulance of the woman he loves. When Dasharatha hears what will make Kaikeyi happy, he is beside himself with despair. Valmiki describes him in a number of extremely powerful images:

> He looked at her as a deer would look at a tigress. He heaved a great sigh and fell to the floor, like a great serpent made powerless by a spell ... The great king, protector of the earth, wept like a man who has lost everything. He was

---

6 Sattar, *Valmiki's Ramayana*, chap. 15.

> so enslaved by this woman that he fell at her feet. But she moved away so that he could not touch them. The mighty king lay on the floor, a place wholly unsuited to him ...[7]

It is not only Kaikeyi's naked display of power that has felled the king. He knows that he is trapped by the boons he had given her long ago, when she had saved his life on the battlefield. The principles that govern the dharma that Dasharatha has upheld as a public figure, as a king, also govern the dharma – manifest as a promise made in a moment of excitement or gratitude – that is now called upon in the most private of spaces and relationships. If he chooses to honour that promise to Kaikeyi, Dasharatha's dharma as a husband will destroy the reputation of King Dasharatha as a ruler wedded to truth, justice and the welfare of his people.

When Rama is summoned to Kaikeyi's chambers to be told of his exile, Dasharatha has been rendered speechless – with anger, with frustration and with guilt.

> [T]he king seemed unhappy, his face dark with grief ... The grief-stricken king could barely speak and he dared not look Rama in the face. His eyes filled with tears, he whispered his son's name and fell silent.
>
> When he saw how upset his father was, Rama felt fear clutch at his heart, as if he had stepped unawares on a snake. He had never seen him like that before. Dasharatha's deep sorrow was evident on his face and in

7 Sattar, *Valmiki's Ramayana*, chap. 15.

> his long sighs which were like the uneven sound of the ocean during a solar eclipse.[8]

Undaunted, it is Kaikeyi who tells her stepson that his father wishes him to go into the forest for fourteen years while her own son rules in his place.

Another perspective on Dasharatha is afforded by his older queen Kaushalya, when Rama tells her – his mother – that he has been sent into exile by his father's wish. Kaushalya's lament at this time is a mixture of her son's misfortune and her own. 'I had neither the good fortune nor the happiness of being my husband's favourite ... Though I am superior to all the king's other wives, I have had to tolerate many remarks from them that have wounded me deeply.'[9] Clearly, Dasharatha has always favoured Kaikeyi whom we, as readers, are led to believe is the most physically alluring of all the three queens.[10] Kaushalya appears to be more of an official consort to Dasharatha, her marriage to Dasharatha a political union of traditionally conservative caste and status, rather than the more volatile union of love and desire.[11] When Dasharatha wanted to marry

---

8 Sattar, *Valmiki's Ramayana*, chap. 15.

9 Sattar, *Valmiki's Ramayana*, chap. 16.

10 Sumitra, who received two unequal portions of the substance offered by the divine creature that stepped out of the sacrifice, and is the mother of the twins Lakshmana and Shatrughna, is noticeable only by her silence in Valmiki's text.

11 This kind of marriage for a king is more explicit in the Mahabharata – Pandu marries Kunti but it is Madri who has his heart. Pandu asks Kunti to share her boon of sons from the gods with Madri, who also desires to

her, Kaikeyi's father gave his permission on the condition that her son would succeed Dasharatha and be king of Kosala.[12] This suggests that Dasharatha was older than Kaikeyi and that he was already married, at least once, if not twice. More and more, we are persuaded that Kaikeyi was the beloved of Dasharatha's later years, a woman who made him feel young and strong and virile. As it turns out, she becomes the woman who causes his premature death. Some of this discomfort with the obvious power that Kaikeyi wields over Dasharatha is expressed by Lakshmana when he hears about his brother's banishment. Lakshmana says to Kaushalya, 'Mother, I, too, do not like the fact that Rama has to give up the kingdom and go into the forest because of a woman's whim! The king is old and senile and succumbs to his lust. Who knows what he might say in the throes of passion! I cannot think of any crime that Rama has committed, nor can I think of a flaw in his character. How can

---

have children. As a result of a long-ago curse, death claims Pandu as he is making love to Madri and it is she who climbs on to his funeral pyre as his wife and his beloved. Kunti, now a destitute widow, must look after all five boys, dependent on the largesse of the Kaurava court.

12 Once again, we must recall the Mahabharata when Shantanu, already king of Hastinapura and father of the magnificent prince Gangadatta (later known as Bhishma), wants to marry the fisher girl Matsyagandha (Satyavati). Her father agrees only on the condition that his daughter's son will be king after Shantanu. Shakuntala, too, in the Mahabharata, sleeps with Dushyanta only on the condition that her son will be king. It is important to note that a new wife will want the king to explicitly state that her son will be king, asking that the monarch go against both prevalent custom and law that the first son of the first wife (or the oldest wife) be the legitimate heir to the throne.

he be banished into the forest?'[13] Later in the same conversation, when Lakshmana declares that he will go with Rama into the forest, Kaushalya says that she, too, must follow her son. Rama gently admonishes her: 'The king is being controlled by Kaikeyi. When I have gone, he will not survive if you, too, were to desert him. A woman cannot abandon her husband. It would be a cruel thing to do and is, therefore, impossible. Put that thought out of your mind. As long as my father, the ruler of the earth, is alive, so long shall you attend and care for him.'[14]

The next time we see Dasharatha is when Rama, Lakshmana and Sita come to seek the king's blessings before they leave for the forest. Overwhelmed by the moment and perhaps by what he has caused, the old king faints and has to be revived. He says, 'Rama, I have been trapped by Kaikeyi's boons. Take over as king of Ayodhya today and have me arrested!'[15] Realizing that Rama is not going to change his mind, Dasharatha again becomes the father who cannot bear the thought of being separated from his son. Putting aside the fact that he has just asked Rama to do something unthinkable and profoundly inappropriate by having him arrested, Dasharatha blesses him but then pleads for one more night in his company. 'But look, it is already evening. Do not leave today. Stay here this one night so that your mother and I can gaze at you to our heart's content and fulfil your every desire. Leave in the morning!'[16]

---

13 Sattar, *Valmiki's Ramayana*, chap. 16.

14 Sattar, *Valmiki's Ramayana*, chap. 16.

15 Sattar, *Valmiki's Ramayana*, chap. 18.

16 Sattar, *Valmiki's Ramayana*, chap. 18.

Kaikeyi is unmoved by the emotional upheaval that is taking place before her eyes. She presents Sita with the simple clothes that she must wear in the forest and the king hangs his head in shame. Rama asks his father to take care of Kaushalya, his neglected queen.

> 'My mother, the righteous Kaushalya, is known for her virtues and she is free of petty jealousies,' said Rama to his father. 'She is old now and she has never criticized you. She will drown in an ocean of sorrow when I have gone. Please treat her better than you have before. Be good to my mother who shall be pining for me ...'[17]

Rama's criticism of Kaikeyi is implicit in the way he describes his mother's good qualities, and he is quite blunt in asking the king to treat his senior wife better than he has done so far. Clearly, Dasharatha's preferences have been no secret, and sadly, he must now pay a price for the all-too-human mistake of loving unequally and too much. But the old king has our sympathy as Rama drives out of the city of his birth towards the forest:

> The king stepped out of his palace surrounded by sorrowing women. 'Let me see my beloved son!' he cried. The wailing of the king's women filled the air like that of female elephants when their mate has been captured. And the mighty Ikshvaku Dasharatha, both father and king, his

---

[17] Sattar, *Valmiki's Ramayana,* chap. 18.

> face was clouded like the moon during an eclipse ... [H]e looked longingly after his disappearing son.
>
> Dasharatha gazed at the road as long as the dust from Rama's chariot was visible, unable to tear his eyes away. He seemed to grow taller as he stood on his toes and strained to catch a last glimpse of his son. When even the dust from Rama's receding chariot had disappeared, the mighty Ikshvaku fell to the earth in his grief.[18]

Now that all is lost – his beloved son as well as his reputation among his people – Dasharatha returns to Kaushalya.

> Kaushalya came and took his right arm to lead him away and Kaikeyi, who loved Bharata best, took his left arm. Even though the king was engulfed by sorrow, he was rich in dharma and retained his natural courtesies. 'Do not touch me, you wicked creature!' he cried to Kaikeyi. 'I never wish to set eyes on you again! Henceforth, you are neither my wife nor even a member of my family! ... You have renounced dharma and seek only material prosperity and so I renounce you! Now and for all the lives to come, I reject that hand of yours that I took in marriage.'[19]

In his desolate palace, Dasharatha seeks comfort from Kaushalya. He says, 'Kaushalya, touch me. I cannot see you. My eyes which followed Rama have not yet returned to me!'[20]

---

[18] Sattar, *Valmiki's Ramayana*, chap. 19.

[19] Sattar, *Valmiki's Ramayana*, chap. 19.

[20] Sattar, *Valmiki's Ramayana*, chap. 19.

Kaushalya sits by the grieving king and weeps softly. But later, Kaushalya gives vent to what she has stored in her heart. She can no longer carry the burden of love and sympathy that the king is asking her to bear. She berates him with the consequences of all that he has unleashed – the difficulties that Rama and Sita will have to endure in the forest, the danger that Bharata might not relinquish the kingdom to Rama when he returns after fourteen years in exile. 'If you were truly devoted to dharma you would never have exiled your virtuous son! You have destroyed the kingdom and the state, yourself and your ministers. You have destroyed me and my son! You have destroyed everything! And your other wife and her son rejoice!'[21]

Dasharatha is then moved to tell her a story that he believes explains his behaviour. It is a complex story and a loaded one. Apparently, when Dasharatha was a young prince, he had the remarkable talent of being able to shoot his prey without seeing it, simply by following the sound it made. Once, when he was out hunting alone, he thought he heard an elephant drinking water and loosed one of his unerring arrows in the direction from which the sound had come. The arrow did not miss its mark, but instead of an elephant it pierced the vitals of a young ascetic boy. Dasharatha was mortified, but the boy was dying and said that he had been the sole provider for his parents who were old and incapacitated. Dasharatha rushed to tell the old couple what he had done and brought them to their son.

---

[21] Sattar, *Valmiki's Ramayana,* chap. 22.

> 'The old man wept as he performed the last rites for his son along with his wife. Then he turned to me and said, " ... [B]ecause you killed my innocent son in your ignorance, I shall place a brutal curse upon you that shall cause you great pain. You too shall grieve for a lost son as I have. And you shall die grieving for your son!"
>
> 'The words of that powerful sage have come true today, dear Kaushalya. I shall indeed die grieving for my son. If only Rama could embrace me now and come back to the kingdom! But I could not have acted otherwise and neither could he!'[22]

This is a most unexpected justification from Dasharatha for what he has just done, that is, exile his son. Rather than citing his dharma as a husband which compelled him to keep the promise he had made to his wife, Kaikeyi, he reaches for karma, his past actions, and pulls out a curse that had remained unknown to this day. The curse, however, does not explain why he exiled Rama – it explains only why Dasharatha must be wracked with the grief of separation in his last days. With this story, Dasharatha is completely exonerated, free of any moral censure, because his present deeds are controlled by a long-ago act of arrogant carelessness. And this, for a king who says that he has always upheld dharma and is acknowledged by others as having done so.

Dasharatha can only save himself from moral censure by citing karma. If he had chosen to say that he performed his dharma as a husband to Kaikeyi, what about his dharma to his

---

22 Sattar, *Valmiki's Ramayana*, chap. 22.

other wives, most particularly towards Kaushalya whom he had just separated from her only and beloved son? What about his dharma as a father towards his eldest son whom he should have made king? What about his dharma as a king towards his declared heir and towards the people who loved and respected the man who was going to be their new king?

The text itself gives Dasharatha a way out of what would have been his moral dilemma. Instead of confronting conflicting dharmas, he has recourse to a determinism from the past that sets him free from having to choose at this, the most critical juncture in his life, the juncture upon which his reputation as a king will rest.[23]

As it happens, no one but Kaushalya (and the audience of the larger story) hears about the curse that binds Dasharatha to this otherwise inexplicable act. And so, in the eyes of his sons (all four of them), his citizens, and for posterity, Dasharatha remains culpable for what he has done. The audience, however, like Kaushalya, is encouraged to understand that karma is binding and to forgive the king for his actions in the present.

---

[23] Dasharatha and Ravana are the only two characters who carry a karmic past into the story. The Uttara Kanda tells about an occasion when Ravana, drunk with arrogance, sexually assaults the apsara Rambha. Ravana is cursed by her fiancé – that should he ever touch a woman against her will, his head will explode. The story of this curse is offered to us as the reason why Ravana never touched Sita in all the time that she was his prisoner. Here, of course, the curse has the opposite intention. It reminds us that Ravana was not honourable in staying away from Sita, he was merely exerting his instinct for self-preservation. Again, we are prevented from passing a moral judgement, and in this case, approving of Ravana's self-restraint.

As Dasharatha and Kaushalya are being reconciled in the palace, Rama shares his anguish about what has happened to him with his brother Lakshmana on their first night away from home. Because he has no idea of the curse on his father, Rama discusses his father's actions in terms of dharma.

> 'When I think of the disaster that has befallen me as a result of the king's infatuation I feel the pursuit of pleasure must be even more compelling than the pursuit of wealth or dharma. Even an ignorant man would not renounce his son for the sake of a beautiful woman. But our father has abandoned me, his most obedient son! ... He who abandons wealth and dharma and chases after pleasure shall soon destroy himself, like Dasharatha did! ... I could easily conquer Ayodhya and the entire earth in anger with just my arrows. But one should never use one's strength without reason. If I do not crown myself today, Lakshmana, it is only because I fear the consequences of violating dharma in my next life!' Rama wept in his sorrow and then spent the rest of the night in silence in that lonely forest.[24]

Although Rama couches his discomfort with his father's actions within the three sanctioned goals of human life – wealth (artha), pleasure (kama) and dharma – he justifies his own obedience

---

24 Sattar, *Valmiki's Ramayana*, chap. 21. However, later, when Bharata comes to the forest to persuade Rama to take back the kingdom, Rama defends his father's actions by telling his brothers about the condition that Kaikeyi's father, Ashvapati, had laid down before he accepted Dasharatha as a son-in-law – that his daughter's son would be king (chap. 26).

to his father's transgressive command by resorting to karma, albeit via dharma. Rama fears violating dharma in this life because of what might happen as a consequence in his next life, thereby suggesting that karma is not only stronger than dharma, but overwhelms it in the long run of many lives. It is not enough to be good, to uphold dharma in this life, for the sake of righteousness alone. It is also necessary to uphold dharma because violating the moral code that has been bestowed upon Rama as a kshatriya could have far-reaching consequences, even across multiple lifetimes.

Whichever way we choose to understand Dasharatha's actions, we soon become aware that he casts a long shadow over his son and the rest of the Ramayana. For example, one of the reasons that Rama is exalted as the ideal man – the maryada purushottama – is because he has only one wife. Even when Sita disappears into the earth, he steadfastly refuses to marry again. We might suggest that, having seen the trouble that many wives caused his father, Rama is determined to stay away from such entanglements. Further, we could argue that Rama rejects Sita at the end of the war because he does not want people to think that he has the same weakness as his father – that love for a woman has clouded his judgement about what is right.[25] The same anxiety propels him to banish Sita from Ayodhya when there is gossip about her among his citizens. The darker shadow, however, is that the weight of Dasharatha's past deeds, his karma, has immediate consequences for his son. The curse that Dasharatha carries is that he will be separated from his beloved

---

[25] See *Lost Loves: Exploring Rama's Anguish* by Arshia Sattar (New Delhi: HarperCollins India, 2019) for more on this.

son and will die grieving for him. That could have happened in a number of other ways which need not involve Rama's exile into the forest, where his wife is abducted and he is pushed into fighting a war to reclaim her.

Dasharatha's karma also causes immeasurable suffering to Sita, who is first separated from her husband, then publicly denounced on suspicions of her chastity, then banished into the forest when she is pregnant, and finally compelled to leave her sons and her husband behind as she disappears into the earth. In the Valmiki Ramayana, we are not aware that Rama's destiny, acting via a curse or any other means, demanded his exile and its consequent trials.[26] Sita, on the other hand, claims that a prophecy declared that she would spend time in the forest. She uses this as an argument for accompanying Rama when he has to leave Ayodhya. She says to him, 'While I lived in my father's house, I was told by brahmin seers that I would have to live in the forest. Ever since I heard this from those men who could read signs, I have been eager to go to the forest. That prophecy has to come true and its time has arrived. So, my dear, I can do nothing else but come with you.'[27]

---

26 There is an obviously later Puranic story in which Vishnu is cursed to be separated from his wife because he has killed the wife of the sage Bhrigu during one of the regular battles between the devas and the asuras. This is briefly referred to in the Uttara Kanda but does not become the karmic residue that Vishnu brings with him when he comes to earth as Rama. Nor at any point in the Ramayana is it offered as a reason for any of his separations from Sita: not for her abduction, nor for her later banishment.

27 Sattar, *Valmiki's Ramayana*, chap. 17.

With his characteristic insight, A.K. Ramanujan points out that the Oedipal conflict between fathers and sons as articulated by Freud is actually inverted in Indian stories.[28] Here, instead of the son destroying the father, it is the father who seeks to destroy the son. Ramanujan quotes the myth of Yayati as an example: King Yayati, who has just married his wife's serving maid, is cursed to descend into old age and decrepitude by his father-in-law unless he can find, within twenty-four hours, someone willing to take on the curse in his stead. Yayati has six sons and begs each of them in turn to take on the curse. Finally, his youngest son, Puru, relieves his father of the curse and Yayati continues to rule his kingdom and enjoy his wife.[29] Following Ramanujan,

---

[28] A.K. Ramanujan, 'An Indian Oedipus', in *The Collected Essays of A.K. Ramanujan*, eds. Vinay Dharwadker and Stuart H. Blackburn (New Delhi: Oxford University Press, 1999).

[29] See also, the Preface in *Yayati* by Girish Karnad (New Delhi: Oxford University Press, 2007) for a further discussion of the reversed Oedipus myth in Indian stories. We can also think about Shantanu accepting his son Gangadatta's terrible vow to give up the throne and be celibate for his entire life so that the kingship is never contested by his sons. By his heartbroken behaviour, Shantanu excludes his son from his natural rights of primogeniture for himself as well as his descendants. Gangadatta becomes Bhishma after he has taken the vow that allows his father to marry the woman he wants and whose sons will rule the kingdom. Bhishma's emasculation to please his father is elevated to the laudable vow of sage-like celibacy. Also in the Mahabharata, Arjuna is persuaded that his son, Iravan, born from the Naga princess Ulupi, become the human sacrifice needed to ensure the success of the Pandavas in the war against their cousins. Iravan never gets the acclamation that is bestowed on Bhishma for what is, arguably, an even greater sacrifice for his father's glory.

we might also see these emotions at work when Dasharatha exiles Rama to the forest, thereby getting his most powerful and likely successor to the throne out of the picture and allowing a lesser son to occupy the throne. We could extend this further to Dasharatha depositing his karma of a cursed separation on to Rama rather than letting the curse, played out in some different way, affect only himself. Rama's forest exile is sure to be fraught with dangers, both known and unknown, and apart from the challenges that the exile itself causes, it could well be that Rama, overcome by these dangers, would not return to Ayodhya.

The most neutral way to regard the effect of Dasharatha's actions on Rama is to see them as the workings of destiny (vidhi). On more than one occasion, Rama remarks that Kaikeyi must surely be the instrument of his fate. The first time he brings it up is in response to Lakshmana's outburst that Rama should imprison the king and continue with the coronation as planned. Rama says to him, 'Lakshmana, you have to see destiny at work in my exile and in the reversal of the kingship that was entrusted to me. How could Kaikeyi have worked against me unless it was destiny that directed her to do so? ... It can only be destiny that has made her act like this. Why else would a noble princess, rich in virtues, speak like a common woman in her husband's presence? That which is unthinkable and which cannot be countered by any creature is an act of destiny.'[30] Invoking destiny as the primary actor in this unexpected turn of events is to absolve Dasharatha and Kaikeyi, even the provocative

---

30 Sattar, *Valmiki's Ramayana*, chap. 16.

Manthara, of any moral responsibility for changing the course of Rama's life.

Dasharatha appears again only at the end of the story – in both endings, as a matter of fact. At the end of the Uttara Kanda, Rama-as-Vishnu returns to his heaven and Dasharatha descends to the banks of the Sarayu along with the gods to welcome Rama. Towards the end of the Yuddha Kanda, when Sita is exonerated by the gods after she walks into the fire, Dasharatha appears in a celestial chariot and praises Rama for all that he has done:

> He lifted him on to his lap, embraced him and said, 'All the pleasures of heaven and the respect of the gods were nothing to me without you, Rama! ... Kaikeyi's words which caused your exile still rankle in my heart ... Your deeds saved me, my child. Only now have I learned that all this was planned by the gods for the killing of Ravana.'[31]

Dasharatha is still holding on to the fact that he was not free to act when he sent Rama into exile. This time, although Kaikeyi's cruel words remain with him, Dasharatha says that Rama's exile was necessary and inevitable because the gods needed Ravana to be killed. At the same time, he acknowledges that he might not have had the pleasures of heaven had Rama not been such a good man: Rama's deeds have saved his father in his afterlife, overcoming both Dasharatha's karma (the curse that he would have to die without his son because he had inflicted

---

[31] Sattar, *Valmiki's Ramayana*, chap. 67.

the same pain on another father) and his dharma (that he chose to honour the promise he had made to Kaikeyi rather than acknowledge his obligations to his son and his people).

Since we know that the Ramayana we attribute to Valmiki was compiled over centuries, we can see that the greatest anxieties of the text are those that are worked on over and over again. As Ramanujan says, 'An epic is like a crystal, it grows where there is a flaw.'[32] As the text coalesces around something like a canonical version, it will proffer multiple reasons for the same disturbing incident. Dasharatha's treatment of Rama is so unexpected because he is known to be a wise and just king. His behaviour must be explained away by forces other than choice and free will. Hence, we hear that not only was Dasharatha bound by previous oaths that compromised his present position, but that his separation from his son was predetermined. In this case of rampant over-determinism, we are encouraged to see Dasharatha as an honourable man, if not as a righteous king. But in a story which is also about the dharma of kingship, this is not enough.

[32] Classroom lecture (University of Chicago, 1986).

AYODHYA'S WIVES

Dasharatha had three wives – Kaushalya, Sumitra and Kaikeyi. Kaushalya is the eldest queen, Dasharatha's consort, as it were. And Kaikeyi is his beloved and favourite wife. Valmiki's text makes little mention of Sumitra, she neither speaks nor acts in the story, though she is the one who receives two portions of the potent substance that the great being who emerges from the sacrifice gives to Dasharatha to ensure the birth of sons. As a consequence of the double portion, Sumitra has two sons, the twins Lakshmana and Shatrughna, each of whom eventually pairs off with another of his brothers, Lakshmana with Rama and Shatrughna with Bharata. Since Sumitra neither acts nor speaks, there is nothing that we can say about her in relation to dharma. We can assume that she was a good wife and mother, perhaps even a good queen, even though her role and position in the triad of queens is unclear. When the queens appear together, for example when Rama, Sita and Lakshmana depart for their period of exile and when Ayodhya's entire court reaches the forest to persuade Rama to accept kingship after Dasharatha has died, Sumitra stands alongside Kaushalya and Kaikeyi, silent but present. Thus, she performs the public duties expected of her.

Kaushalya, on the other hand, presents us with much to consider vis-à-vis her role and status as Dasharatha's wife. The name Kaushalya can be understood to mean 'the woman of/ from Kosala', which is, of course, the kingdom over which Dasharatha ruled. We can reasonably ask the question whether the senior queen got this name after she married Dasharatha or whether this was her name when Dasharatha married her. If the latter, then Dasharatha became the king of Kosala because he married its princess – and that would have enormous implications for the power dynamics in the relationship between Dasharatha and Kaushalya. The Valmiki Ramayana itself does not tell us where Dasharatha came from[1] – when we meet him, he is already the king of Kosala, ruling justly and well from the prosperous capital city of Ayodhya, admired and respected by his people as well as by other kings. Kaikeyi's name tells us that she is the princess of Kekaya,[2] and in and around the Ramayana, we learn that her father was named Ashvapati and that she had

---

1 Kalidasa's *Raghuvamsha*, from approximately 400 CE, gives us a fuller picture of Dasharatha's early life, telling us that he is the son of Aja and that his three wives were the princesses of Kosala, Magadha and Kekaya. Kalidasa also recounts in great detail the incident when Dasharatha mistakenly kills the young ascetic in the forest. Of note is the fact that Kalidasa was writing several centuries after the Valmiki Ramayana, and his *Raghuvamsha* is, in fact, the story of Rama and his ancestors.

2 Sumitra's name means simply 'a woman who is a good friend', or 'a woman who has good friends'. She is the only one of the queens who does not bear the name of the place where she comes from (Kalidasa's *Raghuvamsha* tells us that she came from Magadha). Perhaps this is why she remains unimportant in the story. She brings nothing to her marriage, no kingdom and no grand alliance. Even Sita is referred to often by either her patronymic, Janaki ('daughter of Janaka' even

a powerful brother named Yuddhajit who was an important ally to both Dasharatha and Rama. In the Uttara Kanda of Valmiki's Ramayana, Yuddhajit is present at Rama's great horse sacrifice and is sent home with many gifts and a guard of honour. Equally, he sends gifts to Rama when his escort from Ayodhya returns home. Kaikeyi's maternal family exists on the periphery of the story – Bharata and Shatrughna seem to visit the Kekayas frequently and are, in fact, there when the crisis around Rama's coronation unfolds. They return to Ayodhya to find their brother banished and their father dead from grief. So strong were Kaikeyi's ties to her own people that other Ramayana stories say Bharata was brought up in his maternal grandfather's home. Valmiki, too, tells us, as the Ayodhya Kanda opens, that Yuddhajit had come to take both Bharata and Shatrughna to his father's kingdom, and it is implied that the princes are there for a long period of time rather than a short holiday.

Unlike with Dasharatha and the other queens, we have access to what appears to be a rich and full past for Kaikeyi. In Valmiki's text, when Manthara[3] is persuading Kaikeyi that Rama's coronation would be the worst thing for her and her son, she reminds Kaikeyi of the boons that Dasharatha gave her when, along with Indra, he was fighting the asura Shambara and she saved the king's life. Manthara said:

---

though she, in fact, is not Janaka's daughter) or as Vaidehi ('the woman of the Videhas') or as Maithili ('the woman from Mithila').

3 Some Ramayanas also tell us that Kaikeyi was motherless, and so, she was especially attached to Manthara who had been with her since she was a child. Manthara accompanied Kaikeyi to Ayodhya when she came there as a bride.

> 'During the battle between the gods and the asuras, your husband, the royal sage, took you with him when he went to help the king of the gods. He went in the direction of the southern Dandaka, Kaikeyi, towards Vaijayanta, Timidhwaja's renowned city. The asura was famous as Shambara and knew a hundred kinds of magic. Dasharatha fought in the battle in which the king of the gods was defeated. When he lost consciousness in the battle, O queen, you took him away from there. When your husband was wounded by weapons, you saved him. Lady with the auspicious face, he was pleased with you and gave you two boons. Your husband said, "My queen, these boons will give you whatever you wish for." "I will accept them when the moment comes," you said to that great-souled man. I did not know this, my queen, until you yourself told me a long time ago. Ask your husband for those two boons – Bharata's consecration as king and Rama's expulsion for fourteen years!'[4]

Kaikeyi was clearly brave, quick-thinking and devoted to her husband. How, then, do we think about (if not judge) the outrageous demands she makes of Dasharatha in the twilight of his life – that his beloved Rama, eldest son and rightful heir to the throne, be banished to the forest for fourteen years, and that her own son be placed on the throne in his stead? Kaikeyi had the right to claim the boons she had been given whenever she wanted, and she chooses to do so at a critical juncture in

---

4 Translated by Arshia Sattar, from the Baroda Critical Edition of the Valmiki Ramayana (Ayodhya Kanda 9.9 to 9.15).

her own life, at the moment when her husband would no longer be king and she would become simply one of the former king's wives. As Manthara points out, Kaikeyi needs to secure her own position at the court. But Kaikeyi is devoted to Rama, she trusts his goodness and his sense of honour. She also argues that after Rama has ruled for 'one hundred years', the throne will pass to Bharata as a matter of course and she seems pleased enough with that inheritance for him.

> After hearing Manthara's unpleasant words, Queen Kaikeyi praised Rama's virtues. 'He is a knower of dharma, his teachers have taught him to be restrained, he is grateful, he speaks the truth and he is unsullied. Rama is the king's eldest son, he deserves to be the crown prince. He shall have a long life and he will look after those that depend on him and his brothers as if he were their father. Why are you tormented, hunchback, now that you have heard about Rama's consecration? After Rama has ruled for one hundred years, there is no doubt that Bharata, that bull among men, will gain the kingdom of his father and forefathers. A moment filled with good fortune has come to us, Manthara! Is Rama not more attentive to me than he is to Kaushalya?'[5]

Kaikeyi's confidence that the throne would pass to her son, though unusual, could have two reasons: as she declares above, the dharma that governs kingship in Ayodhya determines that,

---

[5] Translated by Arshia Sattar, from the Baroda Critical Edition of the Valmiki Ramayana (Ayodhya Kanda 8.6 to 8.11).

in time, Bharata too would be king.[6] But the other reason seems more compelling. When Dasharatha asked for Kaikeyi's hand in marriage, her father gave his permission on one condition. Seeing that Dasharatha was much older than his daughter and knowing that he had at least one other wife,[7] Ashvapati asked that Kaikeyi's son succeed Dasharatha as ruler of Kosala.[8] Dasharatha agreed and his marriage to Kaikeyi was solemnized.[9]

---

6 A simpler explanation would be that Kaikeyi assumes that Bharata will outlive Rama and inherit the throne after Rama's death. This would also indicate that Bharata is older than the twins Lakshmana and Shatrughna and that Kaikeyi is Dasharatha's second wife.

7 It is not clear whether Dasharatha married Kaikeyi after marrying Sumitra. Different Rama stories speak differently about this.

8 In the Mahabharata, too, Matsyagandha's fisherman father, also confronted with a besotted, older, powerful, royal suitor for his lovely young daughter, demands that his daughter's son be king after Shantanu. Matsyagandha becomes Queen Satyavati. Because of Bhishma's terrible vow to renounce all claims to kingship and remain celibate even though he is Shantanu's first-born male child, she is able to let her unfit sons sit briefly on the throne of Hastinapura. Also in the Mahabharata, Shakuntala agrees to sleep with King Dushyanta on the condition that the son born from their union will be king after his father.

9 Rama knows about this promise and about the boons that his father gave Kaikeyi. When Bharata comes to the forest and tries to persuade Rama to take back the kingdom that has been snatched away from him, Rama responds by saying, 'Dear brother, long ago, when our father married your mother, he promised your grandfather that she should have the kingdom as a price worthy of her. And then, during the war between the gods and the asuras, he gave her two boons because he was pleased with her. That promise had to be honoured. Your noble

With all this behind her, we could argue that Kaikeyi was entirely justified in her demand that Bharata be made king, even without the boons that she had up her sleeve. She could simply have reminded Dasharatha of the promise he had made to her father. But there is a further argument from dharma that justifies Kaikeyi's behaviour. Kaikeyi was, in fact, fulfilling her dharma as a mother by attempting to secure her son's future in a royal family that had three other contenders to kingship.

We are used to seeing Kaikeyi as the villain of Rama's story, persuaded that her greed for power is what led Rama to be exiled, and eventually, to lose his wife. If we see Kaikeyi's desire to put Bharata on the throne as a mother's natural instinct to protect her child, then we can acknowledge the possibility that Kaikeyi was acting in consonance with her dharma rather than against the various other constraints placed upon her as one of three queens, a queen whose son was not the eldest, and therefore, not rightfully the heir apparent of Kosala.

Having to choose between conflicting dharmas is not uncommon in the Ramayana. On the contrary, these dilemmas are the narrative spine of the story. Dasharatha, too, had to choose between his dharma as a husband (honouring the boons that he gave to his wife when she saved him from death), his dharma as a father (honouring primogeniture with Rama as his

---

mother took all that into consideration when she asked him to redeem the boons. Bound by his promise, the king granted her two wishes. One gave you the kingdom and the other exiled me to the forest.' (Sattar, *Valmiki's Ramayana*, chap. 26) Rama seems to think that Bharata being the heir to Kosala's throne is part of the bride price that Dasharatha paid for marrying Kaikeyi.

heir to the throne), and his dharma as a king (honouring the pledge he had made to his people). When he chose to honour the boons that he had given Kaikeyi, Dasharatha chose his private dharma, that of being a good husband. So, too, when Kaikeyi had to choose between her dharma as a wife (acceding to Dasharatha's decisions and wishes) and her dharma as a mother (securing her son's future), she chose to be singularly a mother rather than one of three queens. This, too, was the elevation of a private relationship over a public responsibility.

Kaikeyi's capacity to execute what she believes to be her dharmic choice stems from her karma, from a single deed in her past. She gains the boons that will allow her to insist on Rama's banishment and the enthronement of her own son because of her act of extraordinary courage when she saved Dasharatha's life in the war with the asuras. On the other hand, the act that changed Dasharatha's future, his accidental (though arrogant) killing of the young ascetic, was elevated into the retributive wheel of karmic justice which he could not escape because of the curse that the ascetic's parents placed on him.[10] And so, like the ascetic's parents, Dasharatha died separated from and burning with grief for his beloved son. Kaikeyi's past karma that later empowers her remains a single act[11] and does not set the karmic wheel of predestination in motion. Because of that, she is free to choose what she does next, and she chooses to act in favour of her son. Kaikeyi is not a rudderless ship tossed about on the whims of the winds that circle her. She talks of dharma when she

[10] The essay 'The Shadow of Dasharatha' in this volume speaks at greater length about why this might have happened.

[11] In Sanskrit, the word 'karma' also simply means 'action' or 'an act'.

speaks of Rama (see p. 47) and is aware that there are rules and mores that must be respected and nurtured. It is within these boundaries that she sees her duty as a mother, once Manthara has alerted her to the fact that she is betraying her own son in her vicarious joy at Rama's coronation.

Kaushalya, too, takes recourse to the dharma of a mother as she tries to deal with the catastrophe that has befallen her. When Rama comes to tell her the news about his banishment, she is in the process of preparing for her new role as the mother of the king.

> Kaushalya had fasted all night and now that it was morning, she was praying to Vishnu for her son's welfare. This devout woman, who always kept the prescribed fasts, was dressed in pure white and was pouring oblations into the fire as she recited the auspicious mantras. When she saw Rama, she rose and ran towards him joyfully, as if she had not seen him for a long time, as a mare would run to her foal. Overflowing with love, she spoke sweetly to her resolute son. 'May you be blessed with a long life and all success, like the other wise rulers of our clan! Your father has kept his word, Rama.[12] Today he shall anoint you his heir.'[13]

---

[12] It is ironic that Kaushalya talks about Dasharatha keeping his word, for he is just about to acknowledge another promise he has made (the one to Kaikeyi) which will nullify the promise that Kaushalya is referring to.

[13] Sattar, *Valmiki's Ramayana*, chap. 16.

Kaushalya is devastated when Rama tells her what has happened. But her first reaction to the news is not that of a mother but that of a queen who has not been treated well by fate or by the people around her.

> Kaushalya deserved all happiness but now she spoke sorrowfully to her son who was attending to her with concern. 'Had I never given birth to you, Rama, I would have known the grief of a childless woman. But the sorrow I feel now is far greater. Earlier, too, I had neither the good fortune nor the happiness of being my husband's favourite. But I waited for the joy that would arise from having a son!
>
> 'Though I am superior to all the king's other wives, I have had to tolerate many remarks from them that have wounded me deeply. Whose sorrow could be greater than mine? I have been insulted while you were still here. Imagine what will happen when you are gone! Life for me shall be worse than death! Even my loyal retainers shall turn away from me because they fear Kaikeyi's son Bharata!
>
> 'From the moment you were born seventeen years ago, I have waited anxiously for an end to my sorrows. I have raised you with prayers and fasts and all kinds of austerities but these have brought me nothing but unhappiness.'[14]

This brings us back to Kaushalya's position as Dasharatha's senior wife, and possibly the reason why he is, in fact, ruler of Kosala.[15] As the first queen, Kaushalya had clearly expected status

---

[14] Sattar, *Valmiki's Ramayana*, chap. 16.

[15] See the discussion of Kaushalya's name on p. 44.

and respect, if not love, from the king. What she got instead was disdain and contempt from the other women at court who threw wounding remarks and insults her way, probably because they knew that the king did not regard her seniority as important. All the power Kaushalya had expected (and deserved) in her position as the king's consort has been ignored. Because we have no backstory, as it were, for Kaushalya, we have no way to know where her own understanding of the respect she deserves comes from. Of course, she has our sympathy as a woman ignored, a woman replaced by a younger and more attractive rival. But despite our sympathy, we are unable to see the source of her larger distress that she so fully and completely places before Rama as he surrenders to his father's decree. The only possible clue lies in her name which means 'woman of Kosala'.[16] As the emotional scene in Kaushalya's chambers continues, Lakshmana vociferously objects to Rama's obedience to the king who, Lakshmana thinks, is too befuddled to be taken seriously. Now, Kaushalya changes tack and reminds Rama that he is a son to her as well as to his father.

> 'Ignore the unrighteous words of my husband's wife. You cannot go away and leave me here tormented by grief! You know dharma and you are devoted to righteousness. Stay here and look after me – that would be the highest

---

[16] It is also important to note that neither Valmiki's text nor the larger Ramayana tradition has chosen to fill out Kaushalya's past, as it has for Kaikeyi, for example. We are left to consider the implications of Kaushalya's name, rather than seek out the explanatory story for her betrayed entitlement. Sadly, in the story as we have it, Kaushalya exists only as Rama's mother.

> dharma of all! ... Just as you honour the king and respect his majesty, so, too, should you honour me. I forbid you to go into the forest!'[17]

Rama has a rather unsympathetic response to his mother's pleas and then her command. He addresses Lakshmana who was the first to suggest that Rama was not obliged to listen to his father. Rama says:

> 'Dharma is the most important thing in the world, truth is established because of it. And obeying a father's command is the highest dharma of all, as is conforming to the wishes of a mother and brahmin. I cannot disobey my father simply because Kaikeyi, our mother, asked him to command me thus.'[18]

Rama dismisses Kaushalya's pathos about her own life as well as her call that he do his duty by her as a son. At the same time, he acknowledges Kaikeyi as (also) his mother and validates her claim to his obedience, even after Kaushalya has referred to Kaikeyi as 'my husband's wife'. Kaushalya is left with nothing but her bitter tears. She has now been rejected not only by her husband but also, effectively, by the son in whom she had placed all the hopes of her resurrection to power. Could it be that Rama, too, realizes that it is Kaikeyi's will that holds sway, not only with the king, but even with the people of Ayodhya?

---

17 Sattar, *Valmiki's Ramayana*, chap. 16.

18 Sattar, *Valmiki's Ramayana*, chap. 16.

The righteous words and exalted moral position by which Rama rejects his mother matter little to her in this moment of her abandonment, both as a mother whose son does not respond to her ultimate plea, and as a queen who has no say in the matters of the kingdom, a kingdom that she might well have brought to her husband.

After Rama has left for the forest and Dasharatha has recovered his senses, he turns against Kaikeyi, and Kaushalya slips back into her role (and her duties) as his wife and his senior queen.

> Kaushalya came and took his right arm to lead him away and Kaikeyi, who loved Bharata best, took his left arm. Even though the king was engulfed by sorrow, he was rich in dharma and retained his natural courtesies. 'Do not touch me, you wicked creature!' he cried to Kaikeyi. 'I never wish to set eyes on you again! Henceforth, you are neither my wife nor even a member of my family! ... You have renounced dharma and seek only material prosperity and so I renounce you! Now and for all the lives to come, I reject that hand of yours that I took in marriage.'[19]

Bharata also rejects Kaikeyi when he returns to Ayodhya. He is furious that she claims to have acted for his benefit.

> 'Kaikeyi, you are a wicked and cruel woman!' he cried. 'Leave the kingdom at once! You have renounced all righteousness, so you can stop weeping for the dead! What

---

[19] Sattar, *Valmiki's Ramayana*, chap. 19.

> did Rama or Dasharatha ever do to you that you caused the banishment of one and the death of the other? ... Go to hell, Kaikeyi! The worlds of your husband are closed to you forever!
>
> 'You have implicated me in this terrible thing by exiling the man whom the entire world loves! You have brought me ill fame in all the worlds! Cruel creature who coveted the kingdom! You are my enemy in the guise of a mother! You have murdered your husband and your behaviour is completely unacceptable! Never speak to me again! You cannot be the daughter of the wise and righteous Ashvapati! You are a rakshasi born to destroy my father's family!'[20]

Bharata's rage against his mother runs far deeper than this outburst. After Dasharatha's last rites have been performed, Bharata and Shatrughna run into Manthara as they come back to the palace.

> Shatrughna's eyes blazed in anger as he dragged the screaming hunchback across the floor. Her scattered jewels added to the palace's lustre, making it seem like the star-studded autumn sky. Shatrughna gripped Manthara more and more tightly and yelled at Kaikeyi.
>
> Terrified of the raging Shatrughna and hurt by his cruel words, Kaikeyi ran to her son for protection. 'Control yourself!' admonished Bharata when he saw how angry

[20] Sattar, *Valmiki's Ramayana*, chap. 23.

> Shatrughna was. 'Women should be protected from assault from all creatures! I would have killed vile Kaikeyi myself had I not known that righteous Rama would condemn me for killing my mother!'[21]

It is clear that Kaikeyi's ideas of her dharma, the right thing for her to do as a mother, are entirely her own. Neither her husband nor her son see any virtue at all in what she has just achieved. It should be no surprise, then, that as readers of the Ramayana, we are persuaded that Kaikeyi is the villain. The story itself turns against her and her accomplice, Manthara, through the angry rejections of her husband and son.

Dasharatha, too, gets his fair share of abuse for his part in all that has happened. After he denounces Kaikeyi, he asks to be taken to Kaushalya's chambers, and there he collapses in her arms. Although Kaushalya returns to her duties as a wife, she is harsh in her criticism of the old king and is unable to keep her resentment of Kaikeyi out of the conversation.

> 'You have treated [Rama] unjustly and now you are ashamed of your actions, great king! But no one can help you in your sorrow! Get up. May your health be restored! The woman who incites fear, Kaikeyi, is not here, so you can speak freely!' she wept ... 'Even if Rama returns after

[21] Sattar, *Valmiki's Ramayana,* chap. 23. It is shocking that Bharata would think about killing his mother, although we have just heard that Lakshmana is willing to imprison his father. Both Bharata and Lakshmana are stopped not by their own idea of what is their dharma, but by Rama's idea of what is right.

> fourteen years, there is no guarantee that Bharata will give up the kingdom and all its wealth … If you were truly devoted to dharma you would never have exiled your virtuous son! You have destroyed the kingdom and the state, yourself and your ministers. You have destroyed me and my son! You have destroyed everything! And your other wife and her son rejoice!'[22]

Kaushalya's rebellion, however, is short-lived. Dasharatha says:

> 'Have pity on me, Kaushalya!' he begged. 'You are kind and loving even towards strangers. I beseech you! You are righteous and know the best and the worst that a human being is capable of! You also know that to a wife, a husband is like a god, whether he is good or bad.' … Kaushalya's tears flowed afresh when she heard the king's piteous words. 'Forgive me!' she wept as she placed the king's hands upon her head. 'You do me a great wrong by pleading with me! A husband who is known through all the world for his goodness cannot debase himself at his wife's feet in this manner! I know that you are an honourable and righteous man and I am familiar with the dictates of dharma. I do not know what terrible things I said in my grief for my son!'[23]

For all that Kaushalya seemed to be asserting herself through a new and more aggressive understanding of how she might act

---

22 Sattar, *Valmiki's Ramayana*, chap. 22.

23 Sattar, *Valmiki's Ramayana*, chap. 22.

and what is owed to her as a mother and a wife, she reverts to being, essentially, the opposite of Kaikeyi. For example, Kaikeyi had no problem when the king demeaned himself in front of her, when he placed his head at her feet, when he begged her to change her mind.

> 'Wretched woman, don't go through with this terrible plan. Have mercy on me! I shall even place my head at your feet!'
>
> The great king, protector of the earth, wept like a man who has lost everything. He was so enslaved by this woman that he fell at her feet. But she moved away so that he could not touch them.
>
> The mighty king lay on the floor, a place wholly unsuited to him, like Yayati who fell from heaven when his merit ran out. But wicked Kaikeyi, the very incarnation of terror, was unmoved.[24]

Kaushalya undoes all the insults and humiliation that Kaikeyi has heaped upon Dasharatha when she accepts him back into her chambers and her arms. She is easily convinced that her anger is shameful and that she needs to support her husband, no matter what. Kaushalya gives up her personal happiness, she even gives up her dignity as a woman, so that she can remain a dutiful wife to Dasharatha and the righteous queen of Ayodhya.

A quick look at Sita's words and deeds while she is in Ayodhya will throw the actions and motivations of the other

---

[24] Sattar, *Valmiki's Ramayana*, chap. 15.

queens into perspective. In Valmiki's text, the first time we really meet Sita is when Rama tells her of his cancelled coronation and his immediate exile. Sita is determined to follow him into the forest, and although she cites the dharma of a wife as the reason to go into exile with Rama, we must not forget that this is in contradiction to Rama's own wish that she stay in Ayodhya, to take care of his mother.[25] Also important is the way Sita speaks to her husband when he says that he cannot take her away.

> Sita was a soft-spoken person who was worthy of affection and respect. But now she spoke to her husband with an anger that arose from her love for him. 'Prince, a father, a mother, a brother, a son and a daughter-in-law face the consequences of their own actions and of what their fate has in store for them. Only a wife shares the fate of her husband. It is clear to me that I, too, must go into the forest. In this life, Rama, a woman follows neither her father nor her son, not her mother nor her friends, not even her own inclinations. She follows only her husband ... My mother and father taught me how to behave in various situations. I need no advice on what I should do now.'[26]

Here, Sita claims to have cast aside all dharmas except that of a wife which is, in itself, sufficient reason to go with Rama to

---

25 Earlier, however, when Kaushalya says that she, too, will follow Rama into the forest, Rama admonishes her gently saying that a 'woman cannot abandon her husband'. (Sattar, *Valmiki's Ramayana*, chap. 16)

26 Sattar, *Valmiki's Ramayana*, chap. 17.

the forest. As she searches for more reasons for Rama to accept her as a companion, she tells him that her time in the forest has been predicted.

> 'Apart from all this, there is something you should know. While I lived in my father's house, I was told by brahmin seers that I would have to live in the forest. Ever since I heard this from those men who could read signs, I have been eager to go to the forest. That prophecy has to come true and its time has arrived. So, my dear, I can do nothing else but come with you.'[27]

But later in the argument, Sita's voice gets stronger and her words hit harder.

> Despite Sita's many pleas, Rama refused to change his mind … Slowly, though, Sita grew angry and said indignantly to Rama, 'How did my father, the king of Mithila and the lord of the Videhas, get you, a woman disguised as a man, for a son-in-law! The world is wrong when they say that there is no one greater than Rama, who blazes like the sun! What could possibly have made you so depressed and frightened that you wish to leave me here, I, who have no other refuge! … I have never even thought about another man, unlike other women who bring shame on their families. Under no pressure at all, Rama, you have decided to leave your wife with others,

[27] Sattar, *Valmiki's Ramayana*, chap. 17.

> the wife you married as a young virgin girl and who has lived with you for so long! You are like an actor playing a role. You cannot go to the forest without me. I will go with you wherever you go, whether to the forest, to perform austerities or to heaven!'[28]

By the end of their conversation, Sita has left all arguments based on the traditional dharma of a wife and fate behind as she taunts Rama, accusing him of being a coward and not worthy of the esteem the world showers upon him. Now, she speaks not as *a wife* but as *his wife*, calling upon the personal contract between the two of them, a contract between a man and a woman who love each other and who have known no other love.[29] Dasharatha's queens do not speak of a past or a present love between husbands and wives in their confrontations over Rama's exile – Kaushalya speaks of duty and Kaikeyi's words are filled with ambition and the desire for power, even if that power is her son's. Kaushalya takes Dasharatha back because she sees his return to her as a final vindication of her own suffering. When Kaikeyi asks for her boons to be fulfilled, she does not mention that she had once loved the king enough to save his life.

---

[28] Sattar, *Valmiki's Ramayana*, chap. 17.

[29] All the usual arguments of over-determination in the epic, such as dharma, karma and vidhi (fate), have been overturned by Sita when she speaks of love as the basis of choice. Over and above the dharma of a wife, she claims love as the reason for her to go to the forest with Rama, a contract between them that even he has to acknowledge. Sita points to the fact that love has its own agency, it generates actions based in free will that could break all boundaries of dharma.

We could argue that Rama succumbs to Sita's argument of love; it is this that persuades him to take his beloved and loving wife with him to the forest. It is certainly the last argument she makes before he agrees that she will come with him. However, being who he is, Rama speaks differently about his change of heart.

> Sita let flow the tears she had held back for so long, like a tinder emitting sparks. Her bright tears fell from her eyes like water draining off the petals of a lotus. Rama took her in his arms and comforted her.
>
> 'Darling, I would not want heaven itself if it were to make you sad!' he whispered, reassuring her ... 'I know I can protect you, but I would never have taken you into the forest without knowing what you really felt. Since you are destined to live in the forest, I can no more be separated from you than a famous man from his celebrity! ... Dharma demands that we obey our father and our mother. I could not bear to live for a moment ignoring my mother Kaikeyi's wishes. I want to live in accordance with my father's decree, for he stands firm in dharma and that dharma is eternal. Come with me and be my partner in the life I must lead!'[30]

This is an odd speech, though not unexpected from Rama, who is increasingly associated with righteousness and dharma in this story. He is tender and loving towards his wife, but he claims that dharma is more important than anything else. He subsumes

---

30 Sattar, *Valmiki's Ramayana*, chap. 17.

Sita's desire to be with him (and his to be with her) into his own chosen dharma as a good son to Kaikeyi and to Dasharatha.[31] But Rama does hint at love, however obliquely, when he speaks of obeying his father's decree which came out of a promise made to a wife whom he loved beyond reason. Rama indicates that Dasharatha, too, has acted out of love for Kaikeyi, as Rama is about to do now for his wife Sita. Acts of love have to be the most subjective, individual choices that anyone can make, for surely, no two people love alike. And yet, Rama feels compelled to transform these acts of will, acts located deep within the sweetest and most expansive spaces of the human heart, into choices that lie within the framework of dharma such as the one that controls him and his father, both as kings and as husbands.

Acting within the constraints of dharma, taking on the roles and walking the paths that have been circumscribed for an individual who is a man, a king, a husband, a son, a brother, minimizes the potential these personal choices have for subversion. Kaikeyi's behaviour becomes determined by her past deeds (her karma) which give her the capacity to demand a dharmic act from the king; Kaushalya's anger is understood as arising out of her dharma as a mother to Rama; Sita's insistence on going to the forest with Rama is predicated on her dharma as a wife. Free will has been eliminated from the discourse of right and wrong, and once again, dharma has been instrumentalized as the basis not only of action, but also of choice.

---

[31] Though not a good son to his own mother, Kaushalya.

THE WOMEN OUTSIDE

It is reasonable to ask whether, in the Ramayana, the idea and practice of 'dharma' exists outside Ayodhya at all.[1] In the city, we have seen Rama and Lakshmana, when they are faced with difficult choices, debate what would be the right thing to do according to dharma. Since their ethical dilemmas are difficult to resolve and the appropriate course of action is not always clear, Rama, Lakshmana and Sita continue to talk about dharma and right action even after they have left the city. On one occasion, Sita suggests to Rama that perhaps it is not a good idea for the brothers to hold on to the code of the kshatriyas in the forest; it would be more appropriate if they were to imitate the gentle lives practised by the forest-dwelling ascetics. Rama himself is troubled by what he sees as the demands of kshatriya dharma, and he rejects it forcefully, both inside and outside the city. And yet, the princes use the ethics they have

---

[1] While it is certainly true that 'rakshasa dharma' is mentioned a few times in Valmiki's text, it seems to be only in dialectical opposition to the idea of dharma that Rama upholds and frequently espouses. More often and more importantly, the rakshasas, particularly Ravana, are described as representing 'adharma', which should mean either the oppositional anti-dharma or the lack of dharma, rather than a different idea of dharma all together.

learned in Ayodhya as the basis for the way they judge the actions of others and as motivations for their own actions. The mutilation of Shurpanakha and the killing of Vali and Ravana are all predicated on what Rama and Lakshmana perceive to be violations of dharma, and they decide that the perpetrators of these violations need to be punished.

In the Ramayana, we know that Rama is exiled into the forest because his stepmother wants her own son to be king. But we also know that as a genre, the epic requires the hero to leave his home, the city, and travel through places that are not only unfamiliar but dangerous. In these places, the hero is brought face to face with alien beings that force him to act in unaccustomed ways. He must either call upon resources of might and cunning that are hidden deep within him, or improvise responses to new situations that are, essentially, threats to his life. The so-called 'hero's journey' is most fully developed and articulated by Joseph Campbell,[2] who spells out the narrative as well as the existential need for the hero to spend time in these liminal spaces where he is forced to confront the opposite of all that he holds to be 'normal' (i.e., what is) and normative (i.e., what should be).[3] The

---

[2] Although he pulls together the ideas of other scholars before him, such as Heinrich Zimmer, Otto Rank, Lord Raglan and Carl Jung, it is Joseph Campbell who most clearly and systematically sets out this theory as a way of understanding the literary character's narrative arc, and by extension, a human individual's potential for growth.

[3] In both the Hindu epics, the Ramayana and the Mahabharata, the exiled prince/king is accompanied by his wife and at least one brother, and hence, the hero is not the only one who is challenged in thought and deed by what he sees around him in the liminal forest.

dharma of Ayodhya is never fully or completely defined, nor is the dharma of the forest. But in both cases, we become aware of the parameters of the particular dharma more through example and incident, that is, by watching how people act when they have to make difficult choices, and through their conversations and declarations. Moreover, Ayodhya's ethical beliefs and practices are thrown into relief by the actions and motivations of the strange and wondrous beings that live in the forest, who follow a different dharma, and therefore, behave differently from Rama, Lakshmana and Sita.

In the city, ideas of dharma often circle around women, how they act and how they are acted upon. And so, for all that the hostility of the monstrous creatures of the forest is focused primarily on Rama, the implications and consequences of their reactions to him rebound off Sita. What these creatures do and why they are punished obliquely tells us what is expected of Sita, as she must live and grow in trying circumstances, away from home, for the next fourteen years.

The first challenge that the exile into the forest presents to Rama, Sita and Lakshmana is the matter of food and shelter. Sita and the princes have already given up their fine clothes and exchanged them for the attire of ascetics, that is, garments made of bark. Their food becomes simpler and more rustic – they eat roots and fruits, and animals that they have hunted. In each place where they settle for a while, Lakshmana builds a hut for them to live in. They remain aware of the danger from forest animals, and Lakshmana is constantly alert.

But the real threat is not the beasts of prey and venomous snakes and insects – it lies in the monstrous and often aggressive creatures that inhabit the forest. Their first encounter with a non-human adversary takes place when the gargantuan rakshasa Viradha charges towards them, his spear spiked with the heads of deer and boar and lions that he has killed. He grabs Sita and places her on his hip, declaring that he intends to make her his wife. The brothers must draw on their courage and their martial skills to kill him.[4] But it is the meeting with Shurpanakha, Ravana's sister, that foregrounds the fact that life in the forest, particularly the behaviour of its denizens, more particularly the women who inhabit it, is different from that of the city.[5] What is followed as dharma in the city is not necessarily normative or even aspirational behaviour outside it.

When Shurpanakha appears, much is made of her unattractive appearance,[6] which is contrasted with what we

---

4 At this point, Rama cries out, 'This beautiful princess, the delicate daughter of Janaka and my lovely wife, who has been reared with every comfort imaginable, is being forced to sit on Viradha's hip ... I cannot bear the thought of Sita being touched by another man. It upsets me more than the death of my father and the loss of my kingdom!' (Sattar, *Valmiki's Ramayana*, chap. 28) Surely, this foreshadows his later discomfort when Sita is abducted and is held captive by Ravana for many months.

5 Katherine M. Erndl writes in some detail about the differences between Sita and Shurpanakha in her essay 'The Mutilation of Shurpanakha', in *Many Ramayanas: The Diversity of a Narrative Tradition in South Asia*, ed. Paula Richman (Delhi: Oxford University Press, 1994).

6 Some Ramayanas say that Shurpanakha first appears as a beautiful and seductive woman and that she only assumes her monstrous form when she moves to attack Sita who, she believes, is the reason for her rejection by the handsome princes.

know about Sita's beauty. Shurpanakha is described as ugly, pot-bellied and cross-eyed. Her hair is dry and coppery in colour, and her voice is loud and harsh. Shurpanakha introduces herself to Rama and Lakshmana by saying:

> 'I am the rakshasi Shurpanakha and I can change my form at will. I do as I please. I wander through this forest by myself and I strike terror into the hearts of all creatures. My brother is Ravana, the king of the rakshasas, and I have another brother, the mighty Kumbhakarna, who sleeps all the time. My third brother is the honourable Vibhishana and he is not like a rakshasa at all. My other two brothers are Khara and Dushana, famed for their prowess in battle. But none of them have any control over me.'[7]

She questions how the two men before her, dressed as ascetics, can be accompanied by a woman, insinuating, perhaps, not only that ascetics should be celibate, but that, unlike her, the woman with them seems not to be independent. The more aggressive and rapacious Shurpanakha becomes, the more delicate and protected Sita seems. Shurpanakha's presence and her behaviour are in direct opposition to the codes of conduct that circumscribe the life of Sita who, here more than ever, stands as paradigmatic for the married women of Ayodhya. As a rakshasi and a woman of the forest, Shurpanakha's actions pose a challenge to Sita's way of life, not only because Shurpanakha is single, but because she is free to express sexual desire, and further, to act on it. The

---

7 Sattar, *Valmiki's Ramayana,* chap. 29.

fact that she proudly states that no man has any control over her indicates that the mores and customs she lives by could not be further from those that guide Sita's life and actions. Whether or not we think of Shurpanakha's actions as being dictated by such codes of behaviour as 'rakshasa dharma', we can certainly see that what she does is not considered inappropriate or transgressive in the world to which she belongs.[8]

As the encounter between the brothers and the rakshasi becomes more hostile, Rama urges Lakshmana to mutilate Shurpanakha, ostensibly because she has moved aggressively towards Sita. In no uncertain terms, he says: 'Lakshmana, you should never joke with cruel and base creatures! Look how frightened Sita is! ... You must mutilate this ugly pot-bellied

---

[8] In the Sundara Kanda, Hanuman flies to Lanka in order to find Sita. He is stunned by the city's opulence and he also notices the beauty of the rakshasa women. He saw women who 'shone like stars, absorbed in their lovers and in drinking ... [women who] were shy and hid in their lovers' arms, like birds clinging to their mates, enjoying a night of bliss. He saw still others on the terraces of their mansions, sitting in their lovers' laps in the throes of passion ... Some were alone, without lovers. Some went out to meet their lovers, anticipating a night of ecstasy, and others were satisfied with the lovers who came to their homes.' (Sattar, *Valmiki's Ramayana*, chap. 46) In Ravana's inner apartments, too, the monkey cannot help but notice that the women are intoxicated and seek physical pleasures with a natural ease. Although these rakshasis live in the city of Lanka (and to that extent are not like Shurpanakha who claims to be a woman of the forest), they are not constrained by the restrictive social and sexual norms that define the women of Ayodhya.

rakshasi, immoral and lustful, without delay!'[9] It is obvious that the brothers' attack on Shurpanakha is also motivated by the unbridled sexuality that she embodies and expresses.[10]

Such behaviour from a woman would not be tolerated within the confines of Ayodhya. Already, in the city, Kaikeyi's ambition for Bharata and her ability to manipulate Dasharatha's devotion has resulted in her being rejected by her husband before he dies and by her son when he returns to Ayodhya. Kaikeyi has stayed within the bounds of her marriage, but her behaviour verges on the transgressive because she has visibly and knowingly exploited what is quite clearly the aged king's physical attraction to her. She has resorted to her sexuality to get what she wants. Rather than considering that the ways of the forest are different, the princes insist on the standards of Ayodhya's dharma as a way to judge and punish a woman who thinks of her own body in ways not familiar to the city dwellers.

Shurpanakha's violent punishment for the transgressive act of asking Rama to be her lover or husband must also remind us of what happened to Ahalya (in the Bala Kanda), who chose to sleep with Indra when he approached her disguised as her husband.[11] 'Ahalya recognized Indra in his disguise but she was

---

9 Sattar, *Valmiki's Ramayana*, chap. 29.

10 In support of this contention, we might note that, in other versions of the Ramayana, the brothers mutilate Shurpanakha even when she does not threaten Sita but merely makes sexual overtures to one or both of the brothers.

11 Ahalya's story is told twice in the Valmiki Ramayana, once in the Bala Kanda, as mentioned above, and a second time in the Uttara Kanda as a story about Indra. In this second telling, Ahalya is innocent of adultery

curious about the king of the gods and agreed to sleep with him.'[12] We might say that Ahalya is not a woman of the city, that since she lived in a sylvan grove with her ascetic husband, she should have the same freedoms as Shurpanakha. But, no matter where she lives, Ahalya is not an unmarried rakshasi but a married human woman, and she needs to be punished because she knowingly (and with some eagerness) slept with a man who was not her husband. As with Shurpanakha, the punishment meted out to Ahalya attacks the locus of her femininity and her desire, that is, her physical body. In Valmiki's text, Ahalya's husband, Gautama, curses her to become bodiless, and in other, later Ramayanas (notably Kamban's *Iramavataram*), his curse turns her to stone.[13] Either way, it is her body that is destroyed (albeit only for a determined length of time). By contrast, Shurpanakha is disfigured forever.

The stories of both women function as cautionary tales for women from the city: as a married woman, Ahalya cannot willingly sleep with another man in order to satisfy her sexual

---

because she is taken in by Indra in Gautama's form. While she might have been surprised at the encounter, she clearly thought that the man she was sleeping with was her husband.

12 Sattar, *Valmiki's Ramayana*, chap. 9.

13 Indra is also cursed by Gautama for sleeping with Ahalya, who is another man's wife. In Valmiki's text, he loses his testicles but is able to persuade the gods that the indignity is too much to bear and the gods attach the testicles of a ram to his body. In other versions of this story, a thousand vaginas appear on Indra's body as a mark of shame for the adultery that he has committed. But again, he is able to plead that the vaginas be transformed into a thousand eyes. It is from this story that Indra gets the name Sahasrakshi, 'the thousand-eyed one'.

curiosity or desire; as a single woman, Shurpanakha cannot express the desire to sleep with a man, whether he is married (such as Rama) or single (as she was led to believe Lakshmana was).

While Shurpanakha and Ahalya raise the question of a woman's control over her own sexual desires and activities, the forest is also home to another kind of woman – the ascetic Svyamprabha, whom the monkeys encounter. Radiant with the powers she has gained from her ascetic practice, Svyamprabha's celibacy is in stark contrast to the sexuality of Shurpanakha and Ahalya.

After Vali has been killed, Sugriva, the new king, calls together all the mighty monkeys in the world and sets them the task of finding Sita within a month. They are sent off in the four cardinal directions, with Hanuman and Angada leading the group that goes south. The journey is hard and the search begins to seem futile. Tired, hungry and hopeless, the monkeys stumble into a brightly lit cave filled with flowing streams, fruiting trees and flowering plants. There are vast mansions with doors and windows studded with precious gems, heaps of gold and silver and platters piled high with luscious roots and fruits. Suddenly, they notice that they are in the presence of an ascetic woman, Svyamprabha. She is wearing 'the skin of a black antelope;[14] she obviously ate very little and she blazed with the power of her austerities'.[15]

---

[14] The skin of the black antelope is usually worn by male ascetics who are advanced in their practise of austerities. Svyamprabha is no ordinary ascetic woman.

[15] Sattar, *Valmiki's Ramayana*, chap. 43.

Hanuman speaks to her; he says, 'Whom do these trees belong to, that shine like the sun? And these perfect foods and fruits? And these magnificent mansions made of gold and silver with windows decorated with strings of pearls? Whose power created these fruits and flowers with this divine fragrance, and the lotuses in crystal-clear water? Are the fish and turtles that swim here really of gold? Is all this your doing? Or has it been created by the power of someone else's austerities? Explain all this to us!'[16]

Svyamprabha explains that the Maya, the architect of the danavas, created the golden forest and the beautiful mansions. He had practised austerities for thousands of years and Brahma had given him the boon of great wealth. But when Maya fell in love with the apsara Hema, Indra killed him. Brahma then gave the forest, the mansions and the resources for endless pleasure to Hema. Svyamprabha herself was the daughter of Merusavarni,[17] and because she was Hema's friend, she was made the guardian of the forest that Maya had created. She tells the monkeys that no one leaves the magic cavern alive but that she would help them escape with the powers she has 'earned from my disciplined life and from the practise of austerities'.[18] She tells them to close their eyes, and when the monkeys open

---

[16] Sattar, *Valmiki's Ramayana*, chap. 43.

[17] The Merusavarnis are the ninth, tenth, eleventh and twelfth Manus, mind-born sons of one of Daksha's daughters.

[18] Sattar, *Valmiki's Ramayana*, chap. 43. We never learn why Svyamprabha shows the monkeys favour and why she uses her extraordinary powers to take them to safety. We can only assume that she was moved by their plight and was persuaded that their mission was an important one.

them again, they find themselves on the shores of the restless ocean.

The monkeys have recently left the women they know and love behind in Kishkindha. The self-illumined ascetic woman in the cave with her spiritual powers presents a contrast to the sexual and conjugal behaviour of the female monkeys. Lakshmana notices the monkey women when he enters Kishkindha at the end of the rainy season to remind Sugriva of his promise to start the search for Sita. There is a subdued sensuality about Kishkindha as we can see from the fact that its roads were 'perfumed with flowers and sandal paste and the fragrance of natural liquors like mead and toddy wafted through the air'.[19] Lakshmana sees that the monkey citizens were 'children of gods and gandharvas and they could change their forms at will. They were beautiful to behold in their fine clothes and celestial garlands ... he saw scores of women, all of them revelling in their youth and beauty. They sat there, adorned with rare flowers and exquisite jewels, weaving garlands.'[20] Women like these surround Sugriva who lolls on a couch with Ruma in his arms. But when Lakshmana gives vent to his anger and threatens Sugriva, it is Tara who speaks up for her younger brother-in-law, the monkey who seems to have forgotten his promise to the princes. She assures Lakshmana that Sugriva is brave and honourable, and that he has already sent for the mighty monkeys who are sure to defeat Ravana. One of things Tara says in Sugriva's defence is that 'Rama should forgive this

---

[19] Sattar, *Valmiki's Ramayana*, chap. 40.

[20] Sattar, *Valmiki's Ramayana*, chap. 40.

obsession with sensual pleasures in someone who has been deprived for so long and who, despite these gratifications, is still not satisfied'.[21] Tara's plea indicates that the enjoyment of physical pleasures is held in high regard by the monkeys.

Kishkindha does not seem to have the strict monogamy of Ayodhya – both Vali and Sugriva 'take' each other's wives when the husbands are absent, suggesting that the customs of Kishkindha permitted such levirate relationships. When Sugriva returns after he believes that Vali has been killed by Mayavi, he is installed on the throne of Kishkindha and takes Tara as his consort as if by right. And even though her husband is not presumed dead, Vali similarly claims Ruma when he sends Sugriva into exile, even though her husband is not dead. Rama declares that he has killed Vali for taking his younger brother's wife, whom he should have treated as a daughter-in-law; in this, Rama seems unaware of (or perhaps simply in disagreement with) the social and sexual mores that prevail in Kishkindha. As Vali dies, he turns his son, Angada, over to Sugriva's care, and then he speaks to Sugriva about his wife, Angada's mother: 'Tara, the daughter of Sushena, is intelligent and understands the subtleties and nuances of every situation. She can see danger and prepares for it. You should follow her advice without hesitation. Her judgement is flawless and she is never wrong.'[22] By doing this, Vali absolves Sugriva of what Rama could have regarded as the transgression Sugriva himself has committed.[23]

---

[21] Sattar, *Valmiki's Ramayana*, chap. 40.

[22] Sattar, *Valmiki's Ramayana*, chap. 38.

[23] It is also worth noting that Ayodhya does not seem to ask its kings to be monogamous – Dasharatha has three wives. So Rama's contempt

For the monkeys who have travelled into unfamiliar places outside their lush and prosperous kingdom, Svyamprabha's asceticism contrasts with, and therefore highlights, the easy, natural sensuality that prevails among their own people, which allows for the more open interactions between males and females in Kishkindha. The ascetic woman's magical powers also reinforce the difference between herself and the women – such as Ahalya and Shurpanakha – who see the body as an instrument and locus of pleasure.

While the search for Sita ends at the ocean shore for the rest of the monkeys, Hanuman travels onward to Lanka before the quest for the abducted princess is truly complete. Svyamprabha is not the only unexpected and unfamiliar woman that Hanuman meets on his journey to find Sita. As he leaps over the ocean to Lanka, he is accosted by two monstrous rakshasis who rise out of the waters, Surasa and Simhika. Surasa stops him, saying that she has a boon by which all that she deems food must enter her mouth. Hanuman challenges her by expanding himself to an enormous size, and when she has opened her mouth as wide as one hundred yojanas, he becomes tiny and flies in and out of her mouth, thereby fulfilling the terms of her boon as well as preserving his life. Simhika, the leonine rakshasi who lives beneath the waves, is also eager to make a meal of the great-souled monkey. But Hanuman simply flies into her giant maw,

---

for Kishkindha's customs is not that its kings are polygamous, but that they take their sisters-in-law as consorts. In the larger belief system that the Ramayana engenders, one of the reasons that Rama is called the ideal man is because he remained faithful to Sita and never took another wife, even after her final disappearance into the earth.

down into her body and rips up her entrails. Hanuman's final obstacle is Lankini, the goddess of the island fortress. Hanuman is unable to persuade her that he is but an innocent visitor to the fabled city and so, eventually, he knocks her over and proceeds with his mission.

The rakshasis Hanuman encounters in his journey across the waters, and later, the women he sees in Lanka, both ugly and beautiful, could not be more unlike the luminous ascetic he encountered in the magic cavern at the edge of the forest. However, for Hanuman, Svyamprabha provides more than a foil to the rakshasis. Her appearance and demeanour anticipate the Sita that Hanuman will meet in Ravana's ashoka grove. In her captivity, Sita lives as a female ascetic would. Her royal finery was sacrificed as she left Ayodhya, long before her abduction, but in the ashoka grove, she seems to have only the garment she was wearing when Ravana carried her away. When Hanuman sees her for the first time, he notices that:

> She was wearing a dirty, soiled garment and was thin and pale from fasting. She sighed deeply again and again but she shone still like a moonbeam in the bright half of the lunar fortnight even though her beauty was diffused, as a flame is dimmed by smoke. Her yellow silken garment was fine but worn and without any jewellery, she was like a pool without its lotuses. Her sad face was tear-stained, her hair hung down her back in a single braid. She was emaciated from not eating, for her grief never left her.[24]

---

[24] Sattar, *Valmiki's Ramayana,* chap. 47.

Like Svyamprabha's austerity in the midst of her enchanted surroundings, Sita's ascetic appearance is in direct contrast to the opulence of Ravana's pleasure garden filled with fruiting and flowering trees and golden pavilions studded with jewels. When he enters the grove that is protected by high walls, Hanuman sees:

> courtyards paved with gold and silver and pearls. He saw pools of different shapes and sizes, filled with clear sparkling water, with jewelled steps leading into them. They had crystal bottoms and banks of coral and pearls. They were lined with golden-hued trees which made them shine pleasantly. Lotuses and lilies bloomed there and the calls of waterbirds could be heard.[25]

Sita's resemblance to women who have renounced worldly ties is magnified by the fact that she is not with her husband. She has given up all the outward signs of marriage that, typically, are displayed in bodily adornments, such as clothes, hairstyles and jewellery. That she seems emaciated from fasting also resonates with the ascetic practices of renunciant women. Further, Sita's appearance directly recalls Svyamprabha (the 'self-illuminated one') when we are told that she 'shone like a moonbeam' despite her physical and emotional distress.

Later, when Hanuman has set fire to Lanka, he is stricken by the thought that, as he was rejoicing in his cleverness, he had

---

[25] Sattar, *Valmiki's Ramayana*, chap. 47.

put Sita's life in danger, for surely, the fire would also devastate the grove where she was being held.

> As he watched the city burn, a terrible thought entered his mind and he was disgusted with himself. 'What have I done by setting fire to Lanka?' ... If Sita has been burned along with Lanka then I have ruined my master's plans because of my ignorance. I did not protect Sita before I set fire to Lanka ... The whole city is in ashes. There does not appear to be a single part that has not been burned. I am sure Sita is dead!'[26]

As he berates himself for his stupidity and his essential monkey nature, Hanuman has an uplifting thought.

> [H]e recalled the auspicious omens he had seen earlier. 'Could it be that the beautiful woman is protected by her own merit? Fire cannot burn fire. A virtuous woman cannot be destroyed.[27] Fire dare not touch this woman who is protected by her own virtue and who is the wife of the effulgent and righteous Rama. In fact, it is because of Rama's power and Sita's virtue that the fire did not burn me either. If he did not burn my tail, how could he consume this noble woman? Sita can burn the fire because

---

[26] Sattar, *Valmiki's Ramayana*, chap. 52.

[27] Obviously, this is the same merit as what keeps Sita unharmed during her trial by fire at the end of the war. It is also clear that Sita knows that her virtue will protect her, because she is the one who asks for this trial.

> of her devotion to her husband, her asceticism and her wisdom!'[28]

Again, like Svyamprabha, Sita's austerities in the absence of her husband have given her the power to protect herself. It is her virtue that is her shield, a virtue born from the way she has lived in her captivity. She has lived a simple life and, perhaps more importantly for the powers she now has, she has been celibate.[29]

Unlike Rama and Lakshmana, who are fundamentally opposed to the ways of living and being they encounter once they have left Ayodhya, Sita seems to have a greater acceptance of these ways and a deeper understanding of the changes that they, as humans, will need to make in their own lives if they are to live in harmony with their environment. Even during their early days in the forest, Sita speaks to Rama about behaving differently for the period of their exile, for the time that they are away from Ayodhya. She urges him to give up his weapons and says:

> 'What a difference there is between the life of weapons and that of the forest, between the vows of a kshatriya and those of an ascetic! We must learn to respect the code of behaviour of the world we now inhabit. Here, the mind is perverted by extreme proximity to weapons. You can

---

[28] Sattar, *Valmiki's Ramayana*, chap. 52.

[29] In Hindu mythology, we are familiar with the idea of celibate sages attaining great powers from having renounced their physical desires. Sita and Svyamprabha are examples of celibate women who also gain special powers from their renunciation.

return to the code of the kshatriyas when we go back to Ayodhya!'[30]

In the forest, Rama's insistence that Ayodhya's dharma should prevail everywhere results in the violence inflicted on Shurpanakha and in the killing of Vali. In contrast, we might say that Sita's sensitivity to her environment indicates that she has glimpsed herself in the refracted mirror that the women outside the city (the sages' wives and Shurpanakha) provide and has recognized the person that she must be while she is away from home. With this realization, Sita leaves the mores of Ayodhya behind and adopts the ways of the ascetic/forest dweller. She does this by rejecting violence and embracing (rather than merely living out) a simple life, never more so than during the months she is forced to spend in Lanka. One might argue that, in Lanka, Sita is merely extending the dharma that she knows and in which she has been raised – that is, the dharma of a married woman who must reject sexual advances and stand firm against physical threats from a persistent and powerful suitor. But the Ramayana ups the ante by emphasizing Sita's wilful asceticism in Lanka and making it the source of power. Hanuman recognizes that power, in large part because he has only recently been protected by Svyamprabha, whose extraordinary capacities arose from her celibacy and the practise of austerities.

The power that Sita derives from her asceticism becomes, eventually, the proof of her chastity. When Rama accuses her of infidelity at the end of the war with the rakshasas, Sita asks

---

[30] Sattar, *Valmiki's Ramayana*, chap. 28.

Lakshmana to build a fire for her. Unable to bear her husband's accusations, she believes that a trial by fire will publicly prove her innocence.[31]

> Sita honoured her husband with a bowed head and approached the flames. She honoured the gods and the brahmins and stood in front of the fire with her palms together. She said, 'If my heart has never strayed from Rama, let the god of fire, eternal witness to all that happens in the world, protect me!' She walked around the fire and then, her mind calm and serene, she stepped into it'.[32]

The gods come to earth and proclaim Sita's innocence and also announce to Rama that he is not merely the son of Dasharatha. Rather, he is the eternal Vishnu. Then, the 'fire god rose, carrying Sita in his arms. Sita shone like the morning sun. She wore ornaments of beaten gold and red clothes, Her hair was dark and curly and her garlands were unwithered. Seated in the fire's lap, she was exactly as she had been before.'[33]

All the signs of Sita's ascetic life have been erased when the fire returns her to Rama. She is adorned with gold, her single braid has been transformed into a mass of curls, and she wears

---

[31] Perhaps it is the same power, born of her asceticism and her chastity, that allows Sita to enter the earth on a throne carried by nagas at her second trial at Rama's sacrifice in Ayodhya.

[32] Sattar, *Valmiki's Ramayana*, chap. 67.

[33] Sattar, *Valmiki's Ramayana*, chap. 67.

the red garments symbolic of an auspicious bride.[34] This, too, reminds us of how Sita chose to live in the forest and during her captivity. Her austerity, signalled in her clothes and her behaviour, has been deliberate and conscious, unusual for a married woman but not for a woman who is responding to the dramatically different situation in which Sita finds herself, a situation that demands a radically different way of being.

We become aware of the significance of Sita's choices when we recall the many and various women outside Ayodhya that have provided a contrast to her – Shurpanakha, Tara, Ruma, and finally, Svyamprabha. Each one presents the audience of the Ramayana with a chance to think about the ways in which this princess and devoted wife has been accustomed to inhabiting the world, and how she must find new ways of inhabiting it as her life presents new challenges. The two women of the forest that are most significant for our understanding of Sita's dharma are Shurpanakha and Svyamprabha. As single women who are radically different from each other – the rakshasi who exploits her sexual freedom and the ascetic woman who remains celibate – they hold up a refractive mirror to the normative behaviour prescribed for married women, specifically for Sita. Both the rakshasi and the ascetic woman claim the forest as the place where they can live as they please, a place where the stringent rules that circumscribe Sita's life do not apply.

But the forest, this liminal space, is also a place of bewilderment. For all that Sita has intuited the right way to live

[34] Additionally, her unwithered garlands suggest her apotheosis into a goddess, no doubt to match Rama's recently revealed divine nature.

in, with and against the unfamiliar, her capacity to unerringly discriminate between the real and the illusory, between what is appropriate and what is transgressive, is compromised with the appearance of the golden deer. She is enchanted by this wondrous animal and she surprises us with her reaction.

> 'Noble one, this deer has captivated my mind,' she said to Rama happily. 'Bring him to me, great hero! He can be our pet! ... If you can capture this deer alive, he will be a source of great wonder and amazement. When our exile is over and we return again to Ayodhya, this wondrous deer can adorn our private apartments. He will delight Bharata and my mothers-in-law as well as you and me! I will be happy even with his skin if you can't get him alive. I would love to sit with you on the golden skin of this deer when he is dead. I know it is inappropriate for a woman to speak cruelly like this out of greed, but the deer's magnificent body has me completely enthralled!'[35]

Rama is equally enchanted by the deer and when Lakshmana warns him that the deer must be a demonic illusion, he dismisses his brother's concerns and says:

> 'Beautiful Sita shall sit with me on the jewelled skin of this incredible deer! I cannot imagine that the fur of any other animal could be as soft as this one's! And if, as you suggest Lakshmana, this deer is the creation of sorcery and magic,

---

35 Sattar, *Valmiki's Ramayana,* chap. 32.

> that it is really a rakshasa, then it is my duty to kill it! ... I am always self-controlled and I cleave to dharma. This rakshasa will die because he has challenged me.'[36]

Unlike his more circumspect wife, Rama declares that whatever he does, his actions will always be in consonance with dharma. Because of this, we are led to consider what dharma means outside Ayodhya, to whom its definition belongs, and who is judged by what might well be its unfamiliar and alien constraints. The liminal space itself is ill-defined, blurred at its edges as well as in its internal boundaries, and so dharma itself is ambiguous here. It is in this forest that Rama makes his mistakes, judging those who live outside Ayodhya by the city's norms. Perhaps, as 'the greatest among the upholders of dharma',[37] Rama has no choice but to insist on the only code of conduct that he knows – the one into which he is born and the one to which he is pledged. On the other hand, when Sita asks for the deer, whether dead or alive, she is aware that she is acting out of character and against her dharma as well. Apart from this single aberrant moment, we have watched Sita slowly modify her conduct, if not her beliefs, in the forest. The conduct of the women of the forest heightens our awareness of Sita's thoughts and actions, and this, in turn, encourages us to look more closely at Rama's deeds and motivations.

---

[36] Sattar, *Valmiki's Ramayana*, chap. 32.

[37] Sattar, *Valmiki's Ramayana*, chap. 67.

THE GOOD MONKEY AND THE BAD RAKSHASA

In the larger Puranic conflict between the gods and their enemies, the logical adversaries of the gods (the suras) should be the asuras (the not-gods). A case in point would be Mahabali, the noble and beloved asura monarch of the three worlds, who was tricked by the high-stepping dwarf Vamana to relinquish all the lands that he controlled.[1] In the manner of Mahabali, Ravana too is more like an asura than a rakshasa.[2] But in the

1 The story of Vamana first appears in the Rig Veda but its later popularity can be attributed to widespread Vaishnava theology in which the dwarf has become an avatara of Vishnu and where Vishnu, in his many incarnations, is more and more responsible for the defeat of such antagonistic beings as the asuras, rakshasas, danavas and daityas.

2 In the Uttara Kanda of Valmiki's Ramayana, where the story of Ravana and his ancestors is told at great length, we find that the text often refers to this family as asuras, certainly as often as it calls them rakshasas, and more often than it refers to them as nishacharas ('night-rangers'), for example. They are also called danavas and daityas, which could simply be for metrical reasons required by the verse form, but it does go further in establishing the point that the Valmiki Ramayana is transformed into a mahapurana with the addition of the epilogue in which Vishnu is in eternal conflict with demonic beings. See *Uttara: The Book of Answers*, translated by Arshia Sattar (New Delhi: HarperCollins India, 2019) for more.

Ramayana, it is the rakshasas who are the antagonists, first in the personal enmity between Rama and Ravana, and then, as the story changes over the centuries, this enmity is elevated to a cosmic battle between dharma and adharma.

The rakshasas of the Ramayana are unique, quite unlike their brethren who appear in the Mahabharata and the Puranas and in the wider secular story literatures of the Indian subcontinent. Outside the Ramayana, typically, rakshasas are terrifying in appearance, bloodthirsty and violent in their behaviour, and extremely unpleasant to encounter. Generically, they fall into a class of antagonistic beings that includes daityas, danavas and asuras, who, often interchangeably, wage a constant war against the gods for control of the three worlds. In this larger enterprise, these 'wicked' creatures are hostile to all living beings. Often, we are told that they represent adharma, which makes them the enemies of the gods and humans in particular, since these inhabitants of the three worlds are the ones most invested in the nurturing of the codes of behaviour, conduct, rites and rituals that constitute dharma, which, in turn, upholds the cosmic order.

The rakshasas that dominate the Ramayana live in Lanka.[3] These rakshasas have ruled Lanka for many generations, and

---

3 Every now and then in the Ramayana, we do meet more conventional rakshasas, such as Viradha, who attacks Sita in the Dandaka forest: 'The rakshasa, with his sunken eyes and huge maw, roared like thunder. His limbs were twisted and deformed, his huge belly quivered and shook when he moved and he was terrifying to look at. This awful creature, who wore a tiger skin dripping with blood and fat, tormented all the forest animals. He had three lions, four tigers, two wolves, ten deer and

Ravana, Rama's adversary, comes from a long line of valiant warriors who have a prosperous kingdom and, as leaders and kings, are beloved of their people. Simply by virtue of living in a city, they are already different from the rakshasas that appear in other texts and stories, who are more likely to inhabit forests and other dangerous and/or liminal places. Though Ravana himself has ten heads and twenty arms, and his brother Kumbhakarna is a monstrous giant, Lanka is populated by many rakshasas who are virtuous and many rakshasis who are comely in appearance.

As Hanuman wanders through Lanka on a moonlit night after his great leap over the ocean, he sees that:

> Lanka had its share of good men who deserved to be honoured and respected, as well as heroes spoiling for a fight. Hanuman saw rakshasas who were among the most intelligent of all beings, others who were devout and pious and those who were eloquent and learned. He was delighted to see that some of them were handsome and virtuous and followed the rules of good conduct. But he also saw rakshasas who were ugly and deformed and seemed to have wicked ways.
>
> Hanuman saw exquisite women who appeared to be high-minded, virtuous and pure. They shone like stars ... He saw other women who were illuminated by their own beauty ... He saw women with smooth complexions, bare-breasted, with skin the colour of molten gold, others with

---

an elephant's head, its tusk still smeared with gore, impaled upon the point of his spear as he came rushing towards Rama, Lakshmana and Sita.' (Sattar, *Valmiki's Ramayana*, chap. 28.)

> skin like moonlight ... Everywhere he looked, Hanuman saw rows upon rows of moon-bright faces, eyes with long, curling lashes and ornaments that glittered like garlands of lightning.[4]

Hanuman is pleased to hear the Vedas being recited in Lanka, but for the audience of the story, it is unusual to be presented with rakshasas who are honourable and worthy of respect and who recite the Vedas. As beings who are antagonistic to the gods, they should be heterodox in their beliefs and reject the Vedas and the codes and rituals prescribed therein. By honouring the Vedas, the rakshasas of Lanka stand out, once again, as exceptions to the rule of their fellows.

The first time we encounter Ravana in the Valmiki Ramayana is when Shurpanakha runs to him for refuge after she has been mutilated by the princes.

> Sitting on a golden throne as bright as the sun, Ravana was as magnificent as the fire on a sacrificial altar. Undefeated and heroic in battle, he was like death itself, no matter who faced him, gods, gandharvas, bhutas or the great rishis. Ravana had been wounded many times in the battles between the gods and the asuras and he still carried the scars from when Airavata had gored him in the chest with his tusks. Broad-chested, with ten heads and twenty arms, Ravana bore all the marks of royalty and looked like a king.

---

4 Sattar, *Valmiki's Ramayana*, chap. 46.

> He was as large as a mountain, had smooth dark skin and sparkling white teeth as bright as his gold earrings.[5]

Lest we be enthralled by this magnificent being, the text is quick to tell us that:

> Ravana could stir up placid oceans, he could play with mountains and he could defeat the gods in battle. He did whatever he liked whenever he liked. He constantly violated dharma. He lusted after the wives of others, he was capable of using every celestial weapon and he was always disrupting sacrifices. He had gone to the city of Bhogavati, defeated Vasuki and then abducted Takshaka's lovely wife after he had defeated him as well. In Kailasha, he conquered Kubera and took the flying chariot Pushpaka from him, a chariot that could go anywhere at any time. He was so strong that in his anger he could destroy the forests of Chaitraratha, Nandana and other celestial gardens and pleasure groves'.[6]

Nonetheless, Valmiki seems to find Ravana irresistible and returns to compelling descriptions of this extraordinary being. When Hanuman sees Ravana for the first time, the monkey is stunned by the raw power that the king of the rakshasas exudes.

---

5 Sattar, *Valmiki's Ramayana*, chap. 31.

6 Sattar, *Valmiki's Ramayana*, chap. 31.

> Hanuman came upon him suddenly, and saw him asleep upon that dazzling bed with his breath hissing like angry snakes. The monkey was startled and leapt back in fright. He fled up a flight of stairs on to a raised platform and settled down there to get a better look at the sleeping rakshasa ... As Ravana exhaled in his sleep, his breath seemed to fill the entire palace. His golden crown, slightly awry, was studded with pearls and jewels and his face was illuminated by his glittering earrings. His broad chest was smeared with sandal paste and his exquisite necklace added to his blazing splendour. A dazzling white cloth, fine and silken, was draped carelessly across his body and his loins were covered in yellow silk. Dark as a mound of black beans, Ravana breathed like a hissing serpent and he appeared like a mighty elephant asleep on the banks of the Ganga.[7]

Hanuman's awe for Ravana is renewed when he sees him in his court after the monkey has set fire to Lanka and been captured by the rakshasa guards.

> Ravana blazed with his own splendour and with the brilliance of his golden crown which was studded with pearls. His jewels were dazzling and he wore the finest silks. His body was anointed with rare red sandal paste. He sat upon a crystal throne inlaid with diamonds. As Hanuman gazed at him in wonder, the rakshasa king reminded him of a rain cloud on the peaks of Mount

---

7 Sattar, *Valmiki's Ramayana*, chap. 46.

Meru. Though the rakshasas had beaten Hanuman badly, he could not help but be impressed by their king. He was stunned by his glory and effulgence.

'How magnificent he is!' thought Hanuman. 'What beauty, what courage, what grace! He has all the signs of a great king! Had he not been so unrighteous, he may well have been the protector of the world, of the heavens, even of Indra himself!'[8]

Hanuman is not wrong to admire Ravana, who is truly exceptional. We might argue that Ravana's powers are far greater than those of the typical rakshasas because, along with his brothers and sister, Ravana is descended from Pulastya, one of the ten 'mind-born' sons of Brahma. Pulastya's son was the brahmin sage Vishravas who engendered Ravana, Kumbhakarna, Shurpanakha and Vibhishana on the rakshasi Kaikasi. Kaikasi offered herself to the sage in the 'dark hour', and so Vishravas said that her children would be demonic by nature. But since Kaikasi had approached the sage with the intention of producing honourable and heroic offspring, she begged the sage to reverse his words. As a compromise, he declared that one of her children would be virtuous.[9]

It is true that in the central books of the Valmiki text, Ravana conforms to various rakshasa-like behaviours such as abducting Sita, and being ruled by arrogance, lust and greed. Also, as noted above, every time we are exposed to Ravana's glamour,

---

[8] Sattar, *Valmiki's Ramayana*, chap. 51.

[9] Sattar, *Uttara: The Book of Answers*, sarga 9.

the text quickly reminds us how wicked he is. Nonetheless, Ravana appears to function in the Valmiki story as a largely independent and unique actor – his hostility to Rama is born out of a desire to extract vengeance for his sister's mutilation, and as an afterthought, out of a desire to have Sita. It is only in the Uttara Kanda,[10] when we are faced with Rama's own full-blown divinity, that Ravana is presented to us as one in a long line of rakshasas who are persistent enemies of the gods and are always struck down by Vishnu. It is in this, the last book of Valmiki's text, that we see Ravana consistently acting against human dharma by abducting women frequently, by raping them, and by attacking kings with whom he has no enmity. He even attacks his own half-brother, Kubera, and snatches away Pushpaka, the aerial chariot. His arrogance and greed for power lead him to challenge even Shiva when the god is with his wife Parvati on Mount Kailasha. This saga covers many generations of his family and their exploits against the gods. As such, Ravana's actions are no longer specific to one story and to a particular narrative situation – they are now generic to his category of being. He is opposed to Rama and all that he stands for, because all rakshasas are opposed to the gods. Rama kills him because, in the Vaishnava universe, this is what Vishnu does to rakshasas, all of whom represent adharma.

We are placed in a precarious position as we try and understand Ravana in terms of dharma and adharma in the Ramayana. In the middle books of Valmiki's text, we can judge

---

10 At this point, we should remember that scholars believe that the Bala Kanda and the Uttara Kanda of what we call the Valmiki text (consisting of seven books) are later additions.

him as wicked because he chooses to abduct Sita, he chooses to go against what we have been persuaded is dharma. But after we have read the Uttara Kanda, we see that Ravana acts the way he does because that is the way rakshasas must behave, i.e., torment the three worlds until their transgressions come to Vishnu's notice such that he is compelled to kill them.[11] In this scenario, Ravana is doing nothing more or less than performing his narrative and cosmic function as a rakshasa. We might even say that it is Ravana's dharma as a rakshasa to torment the three worlds and disrupt the cosmic order.

What, then, of Vibhishana, Ravana's virtuous brother, who, when he was offered a boon by Brahma, asked only that he should always walk the path of righteousness? He was also, by his father's word, the one child of Kaikasi's who would be born into righteousness. If the rakshasas of the Ramayana were more conventional, we might have said that Vibhishana was the one going against rakshasa dharma, more so because he chose to behave in this manner by asking for the boon of always being righteous. But we have been told that in Lanka there are other rakshasas who are honourable and virtuous and even recite the Vedas, who seem to aspire to and follow the same precepts of dharma as the citizens of Ayodhya. Vibhishana goes one step further in terms of supporting the ethical principles that govern Ayodhya when he chooses to fight on Rama's side in the war that will lead to Ravana's death. Rama declares that once Ravana has been defeated, he will place Vibhishana on the throne of

---

11 Sometimes, demon devotees receive moksha, the final liberation from the cycle of rebirth and re-death, because they have died at Vishnu's hands.

Lanka. Normally, we would be critical of someone who betrays his brother and is rewarded for this defection with a kingdom by his new ally, but here we are led to valorize and honour Vibhishana's actions.[12]

Rakshasas frequently embody such unattractive qualities as arrogance and greed – one might say that their greatest vice is that they are appetitive and rapacious by their very nature. But if these qualities are intrinsic to them, and acts that uphold dharma are predicated on choice, how then can we judge rakshasas as being adharmic? Our most basic understanding is that dharma comes to the fore when an individual has to choose between a number of possible actions. One option for how to go forward in a difficult situation is rooted in virtue; it has the potential to benefit someone (not always the doer of the action), and it conforms to and strengthens the order of the universe. This would be the 'good' choice. Another available option for how to behave might be rooted in self-interest, greed or deceit; it could disturb the balance of the universe and might reduce the quantum of good in the world. Dharma, in the larger sense, would be upheld by the former and not by the latter. As such, dharma (both individual and cosmic) is predicated on choice – a person who upholds dharma is a person who chooses virtue and desires good.

If we argue that rakshasas are bad by their very nature (that is, inherently and invariably so) then we cannot judge them

---

12 Rama has already made the same move, as it were, to cement a political and military alliance, when he takes Sugriva's help to find Sita in exchange for which he will make Sugriva the king of the monkeys after killing his brother. A longer discussion of this episode follows later.

as adharmic because they cannot choose to do a bad thing, they simply do it instinctively.[13] Suggesting that rakshasas can choose to act from virtue and for good implies that they have an obligation towards dharma – that is another proposition altogether. It leads us to the difficult relationship between altogether different bases for action – svabhava (the nature one is born with which inclines one this way or that) and svadharma (the good choices one uniquely makes according to who one is). If rakshasas are wicked by svabhava, will they be able to fashion a righteous svadharma for themselves?

The rakshasa brothers, Ravana and Vibhishana, and the dharma they should follow are complicated further by the fact that one of their parents is a great sage and the other is a rakshasi. Which of the conflicting dharmas inherited from their parents should Ravana and Vibhishana follow, if they have a choice? As it happens, one of them becomes completely rakshasic and the other behaves more like his brahmin father.[14] However, neither of these fundamental behaviours is by choice, for the circumstances of the brothers' births have made it such that only

[13] As monkeys have a 'kapitvam', an essential monkey nature, so too, rakshasas might have a 'rakshasatvam'.

[14] Vibhishana's half-brother, Kubera, born of the same semi-divine father, Vishravas and the brahmin sage Bharadwaja's daughter, Ilavida, is also virtuous and inclined naturally towards dharma. Shurpanakha is closest to Ravana's rakshasa nature and behaviour because she tries to seduce the princes in the forest and then seems to attack Sita. Kumbhakarna, the third child born of the rakshasi Kaikasi, is monstrous in appearance but is good-natured, loving and pliable. He is dangerous only because of his size.

one of them could be virtuous in the way that righteousness and goodness are defined by human codes of conduct, that is, by dharma. Once again, we find ourselves confronting a universe of over-determined actors as we try to unravel the twisted skeins of the basis of choice and action.

Once Vibhishana has joined Rama by abandoning his brother, his city and his people, he actively contributes to the destruction of his family and the defeat of the rakshasas. He shares information about Lanka's fortifications with Rama and his monkey army commanders, he helps Rama to see through the illusions generated by sorcery, and he is also instrumental in the killing of his nephew Indrajit.[15] Vibhishana knows that the dharma Rama represents is superior, and so, we are to be persuaded that his betrayal of his brother and his hand in the death of his nephew are commendable actions. Vibhishana's so-called dharmic actions are virtuous and 'right' only in relation to Rama and his enterprise.[16]

---

[15] Vibhishana tells Lakshmana where to find Indrajit to prevent him from completing the ritual that will make him invincible. In some Ramayanas, Vibhishana tells Rama that the only way to kill Ravana is to shoot him in the navel. Rama does as Vibhishana says, and Ravana is slain in battle.

[16] In other epics, notably the Mahabharata, the figure of the warrior who stays loyal to his own people despite the fact that he believes them to be wrong is common. Vikarna is one of Dhritarashtra's sons and he fights along with his brothers against the Pandavas, even though he does not support Duryodhana's behaviour or his ambitions. The tragic figure in the Mahabharata is Yuyutsu, born to a serving woman whom Dhritarashtra slept with. He fights on the side of the Pandavas because he believes they are right, but at the end of the war, he is shunned by

However, we must also recognize that when Vibhishana was offered a boon by Brahma after his years of austerities, he chose to always walk the path of righteousness. Wendy Doniger examines the idea of the virtuous demon at some length in her book, *The Origins of Evil in Hindu Mythology (Berkeley: University of California Press, 1976)*. She traces the antagonism between the gods and the anti-gods/demons through the Vedic and Puranic periods, and says that by the time of the Puranas the demons have been 'thoroughly ethicized', that is, they become subject to the constraints of dharma which dominate theories of (thus far, only human) action and we are allowed to judge them from within the precepts of human dharma. Sometimes, the behaviour of the demon devotee will make him stand apart from his people and he might be punished for it.[17] At other times, grace will strike the demon for no reason, making him realize that he should worship Vishnu. And in still other circumstances, the demonic being who opposes Vishnu attains liberation from the cycle of multiple births simply because he was killed by a god.[18]

The Valmiki Ramayana falls between the Vedas and the Puranas, both in terms of its content and when it was composed,

---

Dhritarashtra's court and is killed by a common soldier for betraying the Kauravas.

[17] The best example of this is the story of Prahlada, who worships Vishnu despite his father Hiranyakashipu's bullying and attempts on his life. Vishnu saves Prahlada by appearing as Narasimha and brutally killing the wicked father.

[18] Later Ramayanas tell us that Ravana achieved moksha when he was killed by Rama.

and as such, we might consider Vibhishana a transitional 'good demon'. It is through him that the shifting and amorphous ideas of svadharma (one's own), sadharana (common) dharma and sanatana (eternal/transcendent) dharma might be explored. After bhakti enters the story of Rama, Vibhishana becomes one kind of paradigmatic demon-devotee, acting against the dharma into which he was born because he has recognized another way of acting and thinking that will lead him to god. In doing what he thinks to be right (rather than supporting his brother despite his misgivings), Vibhishana's idea of svadharma (the duty that he must perform in order to be righteous) coincides with the sanatana dharma (the duty above and beyond all personal circumstance and particular situation which is, in itself, righteous) that Rama represents.

The Ramayana tradition, in which Rama is Vishnu, comes after the Puranic period during which the figure of the demon-devotee is a fully articulated narrative trope as well as a crucial character in the theology of divine grace.[19] Because the demonic being is able to receive and be transformed by divine grace irrespective of how he behaves, he can bring together all the contending elements in the multiple bases for action based on dharma. In the case of Vibhishana, using him as an example of

[19] It is worth noting that as Shaiva sectarianism develops, Ravana gets drawn into its fold, becoming a steadfast devotee of the great god. However, he does not become the beneficiary of Shiva's grace in the more usual and traditional sense. Nor does Shiva help him to overcome Rama. But it is interesting to think about whether Ravana becomes a Shaivite only because the Ramayana itself (along with the Bhagavata Purana) becomes one of the bulwarks of Vaishnavism.

the transitional demon-devotee, we have noted that he is both bound to live righteously because of the circumstances of his birth, and that he reinforces this by choosing to walk the path of dharma when he is offered a boon. Thus, Vibhishana can be seen as fully embodying the 'sva' (self) in both svabhava and svadharma, finding both a nature and a code of conduct that is unique to himself as a rakshasa. Because his inherent nature and how he chooses to live coincide outside what is normally considered rakshasa dharma, Vibhishana is already reaching for a more universal code of good conduct (which we might classify as sadharana dharma). Later, when the reason for his behaviour is attributed to bhakti, the dharma that he seeks is transformed into the eternal code of behaviour based on truth that transcends person, time and place (sanatana dharma).

Once again, we find that we reach a fuller understanding of dharma not by what Rama does, but by what those around him do and aspire towards. In his obviously righteous words and deeds, Rama upholds and embodies a dharma that we can all recognize and honour. However, it is through the choices and dilemmas of the so-called minor characters that we are able to better realize the dimensions and nuances of Rama's own search for spiritual truth and the best possible way to be good in the world.

The dharmic dilemma of the rakshasas is both illuminated and further complexified by comparison with the parallel story of the monkeys, Vali and Sugriva. What are we to think when the younger brother, Sugriva, arranges the killing of the elder, Vali, as a consequence of which Sugriva inherits the disputed throne? Both Vali and Sugriva have committed the same transgression in terms of the dharma that Rama professes – each has taken his brother's wife in the absence of her husband. Sugriva is not punished, because, fortuitously, Rama had made a pact with him wherein Rama would restore Sugriva to the throne of Kishkindha and Sugriva would help Rama rescue Sita. Sugriva is automatically on the side of righteousness once he allies himself with Rama, who then kills Vali on Sugriva's behalf.

For all that Vibhishana's actions become more problematic after he switches to Rama's side in the war, Sugriva seems to be ennobled by his new alliance. He is loyal and heroic in the war, taking on both Ravana and Kumbhakarna in battle. However, both the 'bad' and the 'good' acts are in Rama's favour, and by that alone, they become acts that are dharmic. One could argue that Vibhishana was always 'good', and that his consistent opposition to his brother was based on the fact that Ravana was 'bad'. The same, however, cannot be said of Sugriva, whose commitment to doing the right thing was rather more suspect before he met Rama.

The monkeys that Sugriva commands after Vali's death are nervous about his temperament. Even when he is with Rama, Sugriva shows himself to be cowardly, paranoid and not terribly reliable. When the princes first enter Kishkindha, Sugriva and his friends see them from the top of the Rishyamuka mountain. Immediately, Sugriva assumes that they are spies sent by Vali.

> Sugriva saw those two mighty heroes as they approached the vicinity of the Rishyamuka mountain and his mind was filled with dread. He noticed that the brothers were well armed and that made him very suspicious. Deeply

> disturbed, he looked around him but could not find a place to hide. Keeping an eye on the heroes, he found that he was restless, unable to sit in one place or decide what to do, and fear gripped his heart. Agitated and confused, Sugriva discussed the matter with his companions and explained to them why he was so frightened.
>
> 'Those two men have definitely been sent here by Vali to spy on us! They are wearing these rough clothes and wandering in the forests just to hide their identity!'[20]

Hanuman is able to calm Sugriva, who then sends the great monkey to find out more about the strangers.

After Vali has been killed, Sugriva promises to bring the mighty monkeys together and begin the search for Sita once the rains have ended. But when the season of rain has passed, Sugriva shows no signs of honouring his promise. Rama is incensed and sends Lakshmana to the city of Kishkindha to force Sugriva to act. Lakshmana finds the newly installed king of the monkeys lolling about with his women.

> [H]e saw Sugriva sitting on a golden couch covered by a priceless brocade, shining like the sun. Around him sat beautiful women adorned with flowers and jewels. In his fine clothes and celestial jewels and garlands of flowers, Sugriva appeared like Indra himself as he sat with Ruma in his arms. The golden monkey stared at indomitable Lakshmana with his large eyes.

---

[20] Sattar, *Valmiki's Ramayana*, chap. 35.

> Sugriva was terribly agitated when he realized that Lakshmana had entered the palace unhindered. He saw that Lakshmana was breathing heavily and was blazing with splendour, that he was clearly angry about his brother's suffering. Sugriva leapt up from his seat and his women rose with him, making him seem like the moon surrounded by stars in the sky. He stood trembling before Lakshmana, his eyes red and his palms joined.[21]

An obviously terrified Sugriva apologizes profusely and says that he has already sent for the great monkeys who will undertake the search for the missing princess.

It is young Angada, Vali's son and heir, who provides the most damning indictment of Sugriva when the monkeys are far from Kishkindha and have become dispirited in their search for Sita. Uneasy about returning to Kishkindha unsuccessful, Angada foments a mutiny. He says to the other monkeys:

> 'Sugriva is our king and he is ruthless. He will definitely kill us if we return unsuccessful ... It is better to die here, fasting, than to die at his hands. It was not Sugriva who made me the heir, it was Rama! Sugriva was our sworn enemy before this and now he is our master! I am sure he will not hesitate to inflict a terrible punishment upon me!'[22]

---

21 Sattar, *Valmiki's Ramayana*, chap. 40.

22 Sattar, *Valmiki's Ramayana*, chap. 43.

When Hanuman tries to persuade Angada to stay loyal to his uncle, Angada's outburst is even more incriminating.

> 'Steadiness, purity of mind, compassion, resolution and courage are all virtues that Sugriva lacks!' he replied. 'How can he know and love dharma when he takes his elder brother's chief queen as his own, even while his brother is alive? He should regard her as a mother! How can he know dharma when he blocked the entrance to the cave while his brother was engaged in combat? How can he be honourable when he made a pact with Rama and after gaining his own ends, forgot about his part of the bargain?
>
> 'He ordered the search for Sita because he was terrified of Lakshmana, not because he was reluctant to violate dharma! How can it be said that he loves dharma? How can a noble and well-born kinsman trust this creature who is fickle and ungrateful, conveniently forgetting the favours that he receives? ... How will Sugriva tolerate the continued presence of his enemy's son? Why should I go and live in Kishkindha, weak, vulnerable, powerless and without a friend, especially when I have failed in the task assigned to me?
>
> 'Sugriva is ruthless, deceitful and cruel. He will at least have me imprisoned as a lesser punishment in order to keep the kingdom!'[23]

[23] Sattar, *Valmiki's Ramayana,* chap. 43.

Both Angada and Vali invoke dharma at moments of crisis. But while Vali looks to a dharma that belongs to the monkeys as a justification for his deeds, Angada seems to refer to the dharma that Rama upholds, one that prohibits the taking of another's wife and one that honours a given word.[24]

In the Valmiki Ramayana, it becomes increasingly difficult to define a dharma that belongs to either the monkeys or the rakshasas or even to excavate the ethical principles by which they think they should live. In the case of the rakshasas, we have Ravana and Vibhishana acting in diametrically opposed ways, each believing himself to be right. In the case of the monkeys, we have Vali citing the dharma of monkeys which justifies his behaviour, but both his son Angada and his brother Sugriva seem to espouse the new dharma they encounter via Rama. We could argue that, once the monkeys have met Rama, they begin to live by the dharma that he upholds and stands for. As Vali dies, he questions Rama, asking how he could have killed a monkey, a creature with whom he had no enmity and, moreover, while he was fighting someone else. Rama replies to Vali with great anger and justifies all that he has done as a consequence of his adherence to the dharma of the Ikshvakus. He says:

> 'This earth with its mountains and forests belongs to the Ikshvakus. They have the right to praise or condemn all the birds, beasts and men who inhabit it! It is ruled by the

[24] In an irony that we are compelled to note, when Angada condemns Sugriva as being in violation of dharma, he points to the same transgressions that his own father committed (taking another's wife) and which led Rama to kill him.

righteous and honourable Bharata. He is learned in the principles of dharma, artha and kama and he is devoted to justice. We and other kings execute his orders which are rooted in dharma, here and all over the earth so that the eternal dharma may flourish. When the earth is ruled by the righteous and honourable Bharata it is not possible for anyone anywhere to violate dharma and not be punished for it.

'You have transgressed the bounds of dharma. Your conduct is inappropriate because you are ruled entirely by pleasure.[25] You are not fit to be a king! ... A younger brother and a virtuous student are regarded as equal to a son, according to the dictates of dharma.

'Monkey, the dharma followed by truly good men is subtle and hard to understand. How can a fickle creature like you, who learns from other equally fickle monkeys, know anything? Blind men learn nothing from confronting each other! Let me explain things to you. Control yourself and listen to me!

'Here is the first reason for my killing you. You have rejected the eternal dharma and slept with your brother's wife. You lust for Ruma and sleep with her even though

---

[25] On his first night away from the city, Rama cannot hold back his tears as he tries to understand what has happened to him. He says, 'When I think of the disaster that has befallen me as a result of the king's infatuation I feel the pursuit of pleasure must be even more compelling than the pursuit of wealth or dharma.' (Sattar, *Valmiki's Ramayana*, chap. 21) Clearly, the idea of a king who places pleasure above all else is something that haunts Rama. He criticizes his father for this, and now, he criticizes Vali for the same thing.

> Sugriva is still alive. This is unacceptable because you should treat her as a daughter-in-law. I killed you for sleeping with your brother's wife and because you were motivated by lust! There can be no other punishment for this violation of dharma and of the worldly code ... My friendship with Sugriva is equal to my love for Lakshmana. Our pact is that I will restore to him his wife and his kingdom and in return for that, he will devote himself to my interests. I gave him my word on this in front of the other monkeys. How could I then not fulfil my promise?[26] It is the duty of a righteous man to help his friend. All the reasons I have given you are rooted in dharma. You have to agree that you have been justly punished! Stop your laments! You were killed because dharma demanded it. We cannot act as we please!'[27]

Rama's speech to Vali makes it clear that he is calling on a dharma that belongs to the Ikshvakus, one that he is beholden to protect. This is the same, apparently, as an 'eternal dharma' and must be followed by all those who live on earth, the extended domain of this ruling family. Monkeys are incapable of understanding this dharma and have to be taught what it is by other, evidently superior, beings. By extension, once Rama has defeated Ravana and brought Lanka into the circle of vassalage to Kosala, the rakshasas will also have to submit to the dharma

---

[26] Here, too, I believe we can see Rama thinking of his father and his promise, made in public, of crowning Rama the new king of Kosala. As we know, that promise was subsequently broken.

[27] Sattar, *Valmiki's Ramayana*, chap. 38.

of the Ikshvakus.[28] In this scenario, the story of Rama is not about the pursuit of righteousness at great personal cost, it is the story of empire and the propagation of a particular way of being. Rama is not only the upholder of dharma, but also the instrument of its dissemination.

It would also appear that this dharma of the Ikshvakus is predicated almost entirely on the personal moral integrity of the king himself, as we have seen from Rama's criticism of Vali and his implied criticism of his father. Most crucially, the king must be above the pursuit of pleasure as it relates to women.[29] Dasharatha, Vali and Ravana have all betrayed their commitment to this so-called 'eternal dharma' because of their attachment to women – Vali and Ravana taking the wives of others, and Dasharatha being inordinately attached to one of his three wives.

Rama has the opportunity to talk about the dharma of a king when he is in the forest. Perhaps the distance from the city and from the chores of royal protocol has given him a chance to reflect on the destiny that he has forsaken. As Rama, Sita and

---

[28] We can assume that both Kishkindha and Lanka pledge allegiance to Kosala under their new kings, Sugriva and Vibhishana, respectively, by the fact that Sugriva and Vibhishana come back to Ayodhya with Rama for his coronation which is attended by other kings as well. In some Rama stories, Sugriva marches with the horse that Rama sends out during his ashvamedha sacrifice.

[29] On his first night in exile from Ayodhya, Rama says to Lakshmana, 'Even an ignorant man would not renounce his son for the sake of a beautiful woman ... He who abandons wealth and dharma and chases after pleasure shall soon destroy himself, like Dasharatha did!' (Sattar, *Valmiki's Ramayana*, chap. 21)

Lakshmana begin to settle into their exile, Bharata arrives with an enormous entourage. Before Bharata can say that he has come to return the kingdom to his elder brother, Rama asks about the welfare of their mothers and whether Bharata has been able to step easily into his new role as king. He asks Bharata if he is performing all his royal duties appropriately, such as appointing the right advisers and army commanders, dealing with vassal kings, making sure that the granary and treasury are well stocked, and keeping elders and children happy. Rama comes to the end of his speech about the many things to which a king needs to be attentive and then he says:

> 'Do not pursue dharma at the expense of material gain or power at the cost of dharma or neglect them both out of a desire for pleasure ... Avoid the flaws that mar the personality of a great king, including atheism, untruth, anger, licentiousness and procrastination.'[30]

After Bharata declares that he has renounced the kingdom that was bequeathed to him as a result of his mother's boons, the brahmin Jabali encourages Rama to ignore his father's wishes and go back to Ayodhya as king. Rama responds to him with an impassioned plea about the importance of cleaving to truth. He speaks of a personal truth (satya) that should guide all men through their lives, a truth that seems to be higher than the common codes[31] of conduct that constitute dharma. Rama says:

---

[30] Sattar, *Valmiki's Ramayana,* chap. 25.

[31] Obviously, common to people who share a caste.

'The man who lives without restraints walks an unrighteous path. He does not live in accordance with our sacred teachings and he shall never have the respect of good men. It is a man's character and his deeds that determine whether he is high- or low-born, pure or impure, brave or simply a hoax.

'The timeless rules of kingship are bound by truth and compassion. Truth is the mainstay of kingship and the world is established in truth. The gods and sages declare truth to be the highest goal. It is supreme in the world and exalts one to heaven. Men despise a liar as they despise snakes. Truth controls the world and is the only refuge. It is the basis of everything. Nothing is greater than truth. Gift giving, sacrifices, penances, good deeds, even the Vedas, are established in truth and, therefore, it is the highest good.

'How can I fail to carry out my father's promise when I am committed to it by an oath of truth? I cannot violate my father's bond with truth out of greed, delusion or even out of ignorance! ... It is clear to me that every man must hold to the truth, that it is his dharma. It is for this reason alone that ascetics command so much respect. I renounce the dharma of a kshatriya because it is fundamentally unrighteous even though it has some good things about it. It attracts the base, the cruel, the greedy and those inclined to be wicked.'[32]

---

32 Sattar, *Valmiki's Ramayana*, chap. 26.

Again, we see that for Rama, the fulcrum of good and honourable kingship is the renunciation of sensual pleasures.[33] He says as much to Bharata and reiterates his distaste for the pursuit of pleasure when he responds to Jabali.

What is unexpected is how Rama takes the adherence to truth to be, somehow, against the dharma of a kshatriya. Does he mean that any codified dharma, of which kshatriya dharma is only one example, stands in the way of the quest for a personal truth? Do ascetics command respect because they live outside the conventional definitions of dharma, guided to righteousness and virtue only by the truth they have found?

This is not the only time that Rama rejects kshatriya dharma. The first time we hear him speak against this code into which he has been born is when Lakshmana tells him he has no need to listen to Dasharatha's command which exiles him to the forest. Lakshmana suggests that Rama imprison the old king and take the throne that is rightfully his. Rama reprimands him gently and says:

> 'Dharma is the most important thing in the world, truth is established because of it. And obeying a father's command is the highest dharma of all, as is conforming to the wishes of a mother and brahmin. I cannot disobey my father simply because Kaikeyi, our mother, asked him to command me thus. Give up your ignoble ideas inspired by

---

[33] Arguably, it is by this very definition of kingship, a commitment to public duty over attachment to one's wife, that Rama renounces Sita after she has been held captive by Ravana. See more on this in Sattar, *Lost Loves: Exploring Rama's Anguish.*

> the duties of a kshatriya! Follow my example. Take refuge in dharma and not in violence.'[34]

This declaration does not make Rama's stand on dharma and truth any clearer because here he seems to say that dharma is what establishes truth. In the forest, in the presence of the brahmins and his father's court, he says that seeking truth *is* dharma. In the first instance, I believe, Rama is saying that dharma is higher than truth, and in the second, he says that truth is above all, and because it is fundamentally the same as dharma, it should be the absolute goal for an individual's life.

Whatever Rama seeks for himself, and however it is that he defines the path of righteousness for his own life, the dharma that he publicly upholds is that of Ayodhya and that of a kshatriya. This is most apparent when he is outside the city and comes into contact with beings who have an entirely different set of mores. Witness Rama's irate censure of Vali, who has the audacity to criticize him even with his dying breath. As discussed above, Rama kills Vali for his violations of dharma as a king (exiling his younger brother and taking his brother's wife), and in doing so, upholds the dharma of Ayodhya, which is safeguarded by Bharata as he rules all of Kosala. But Rama also argues that, though he shot Vali in the back while he was engaged with another opponent, and though monkeys are not animals that can be killed by kings while hunting, he was still acting as a royal kshatriya should.

---

[34] Sattar, *Valmiki's Ramayana*, chap. 16.

Vali says, 'You have killed an innocent creature like me! How will you justify this disgraceful act to good men? My skin cannot be used by men of virtue, my hair and bones are forbidden to them and my flesh cannot be eaten by those who practise dharma. Of all the five-toed animals, the brahmin and the kshatriya can only eat the rhino, the porcupine, the alligator, the rabbit and the turtle. You have killed me, a five-toed animal, whose skin and bones no virtuous man will touch and whose flesh is forbidden.'[35]

And Rama replies, 'Traps and ropes and snares of all kinds are used to capture animals. Animals are caught and killed when they are running away, or when they are agitated, even when they have no idea of the danger they are in. Men kill animals for their flesh even when their faces are turned away. There is nothing wrong with that! Royal sages, learned in dharma, go hunting. I killed you with an arrow, monkey. Whether you were in a position to fight back or not is irrelevant, for you are nothing but an animal!'[36]

We can be less troubled by Rama's idea of dharma when he is among his own people, but when he meets 'others' (who may follow other dharmas) and physically or verbally assaults them on the basis of the dharma that he upholds, we are called upon to try and understand his behaviour more fully. From his reactions to the rakshasas and monkeys, particularly to Ravana and Vali, we can see that Rama believes them to be adharmic (without dharma, as against simply having a dharma different

---

[35] Sattar, *Valmiki's Ramayana*, chap. 38.

[36] Sattar, *Valmiki's Ramayana*, chap. 38.

from his). Vibhishana and Sugriva, the rakshasa and the monkey who are willing to adopt the dharma that Rama carries with him, are not seen as hostile or deserving of punishment.

Dharma is what Rama does; he is its exemplar. Unlike in the Mahabharata, where dharma is embodied in multiple characters and situations, there is only one man in the Ramayana who lives dharma. The actions and thoughts of all other characters are judged against his conduct. And so it is that we circle back to the idea of Rama as the maryada purushottama. Rama is the ideal man not in the sense that he does not make mistakes; he is the ideal man because it is he against whom all others are judged.

LAKSHMANA SEEKS THE LIMITS

By birth, Lakshmana is Rama's half-brother, born to Dasharatha's silent wife Sumitra as one of a pair of twins. Rather than sharing a life with his twin Shatrughna (who forms a narrative pair with Kaikeyi's son Bharata), Lakshmana forms an almost umbilical bond with Rama. He goes into exile with him and stays by his side when Rama reclaims the throne and rules from Ayodhya. Later additions to Valmiki's text and other versions of the Ramayana give Lakshmana a wife, Urmila, Sita's sister. Even she is left behind in Lakshmana's unswerving loyalty and devotion to his brother. In Valmiki's text, Urmila is not mentioned after the brothers return from exile and it is quite clear that, though Rama is no longer in physical danger, Lakshmana still places his attachment to his older brother above all his other relationships.

There have been many attempts to explain the symbiotic relationship between Rama and Lakshmana in terms of the epic narrative. One, that Rama and Lakshmana form a composite hero, each doing what the other cannot. For example, we often see Lakshmana channelling the anger that Rama must surely feel, as well as taking on the increasing levels of violence and aggression needed to overcome dangerous opponents.[1] The episode with Shurpanakha demonstrates Lakshmana's willingness to protect Rama from executing the extreme violence that the encounter demands. Shurpanakha moves to attack Sita after being teased by the brothers.

> Her eyes blazing like fire, Shurpanakha charged towards the gentle-eyed Sita, like malignant planets circling the Rohini constellation. But Rama stopped her headlong rush. 'Lakshmana, you should never joke with cruel and base creatures! Look how frightened Sita is!' he cried. 'You must mutilate this ugly pot-bellied rakshasi, immoral and lustful, without delay!' Angrily, Lakshmana pulled out his sword and cut off Shurpanakha's ears and nose.[2]

One could argue that the responsibility for Shurpanakha's horrible mutilation actually lies with Rama because he is the one who incited (instructed, perhaps) Lakshmana to disfigure the rakshasi. But it is still Lakshmana who performs the act of cutting off her nose and ears.

The most striking example of Lakshmana expressing Rama's anger is in Kishkindha,[3] when Sugriva appears to have forgotten his promise to call together the great monkeys and start the

---

1 In some Buddhist Ramayanas, Rama is a bodhisattva and so Lakshmana takes on the violence that Rama should perform so that his brother, the bodhisattva, remains free of karmic residue.

2 Sattar, *Valmiki's Ramayana*, chap. 29.

3 It is true that Lakshmana is also enraged when Rama is exiled to the forest, but the anger that he expresses in that episode in the Ayodhya Kanda seems to be his own rather than his brother's.

search for Sita. After Vali's death, Rama and Sugriva had agreed that the monkeys would be sent to the four corners of the world to find Sita as soon as the rains stopped. Rama spends these months that seem like years in a cave, pining for his beloved wife. But when the rains end, there is no sign of any action from Sugriva. Rama says to Lakshmana:

> 'Go to Kishkindha and find that idiot king of the monkeys! Give him this message from me … "The best of men stick to their word, whether it is given rightly or wrongly. Obviously, you want to see me draw my bow, decorated with gold, that flashes like lightning on the battlefield! You wish to hear again the thunderous resonance of my bowstring as I draw it back in anger! … The road that Vali took is not yet closed! Stick to your commitment, Sugriva, and do not follow Vali down that path! I killed Vali with a single arrow. I can also kill you and your entire family!" You know what is appropriate, Lakshmana! Tell him whatever else you like …'[4]

Rama sends this stern and aggressive message to Sugriva but it is Lakshmana who explodes with anger when he sees Sugriva immersed in sensual pleasures, uncaring of what the princes have had to suffer in the previous few months.

> 'You are a base and ungrateful liar, monkey! You made use of Rama's skills and you have not repaid him! If you have

---

4 Sattar, *Valmiki's Ramayana*, chap. 39.

> any memory of what Rama did for you, you should now be making efforts to find Sita! You have indulged in all these vulgar pleasures and you have broken your promise. Rama did not recognize you for what you are, a snake imitating a frog! Moved by pity, the great-souled Rama secured the monkey kingdom for you, you wretched creature!'[5]

One might say that Lakshmana functions as Rama's alter ego, a familiar and effective literary trope where one character acts out the more troublesome aspects of another character's personality.

On the other hand, there is more than one occasion when Lakshmana persuades Rama to control the anger that threatens to overwhelm him. One such moment is when the brothers return from chasing the golden deer deep into the forest to find Sita missing and their little hut in disarray. Rama sees crushed flowers and bits of Sita's broken jewellery scattered nearby and surmises that mighty rakshasas have fought over Sita.

> 'My hostility towards the rakshasas has now multiplied a hundred times. I shall kill all these form-changing rakshasas! If Sita has been devoured or abducted, Lakshmana, there is no one in all the worlds who would dare challenge me! Perhaps the gods think I am a weakling because I am gentle and compassionate and devoted to the well-being of all creatures! Even this virtue has become a flaw in my character! But today I will show the rakshasas and all the

5 Sattar, *Valmiki's Ramayana*, chap. 40.

> other creatures my true powers! … I shall stop the planets in their orbits, obstruct the course of the moon, destroy the fire and the wind, eclipse the radiance of the sun … If the gods do not deliver Sita to me unharmed, they will see the kind of destruction I can wreak in a single hour! There will not be a single god, danava, daitya, pishacha or rakshasa left when I have finished destroying the three worlds in my anger. Even as old age, sickness, death and fate cannot be escaped, so, too, I cannot be diverted from my purpose!' … Lakshmana had never seen Rama so angry before. His mouth dry with fear, he joined his palms and said, 'Rama, you have always been gentle and compassionate and devoted to the welfare of all creatures. Do not let your anger control you and make you act against your natural disposition … You cannot destroy the worlds because of the crimes of a single person. Great kings mete out punishments judiciously and dispassionately.'[6]

Lakshmana's words calm Rama, who then turns to his brother for advice about how best to find his missing beloved. Even when Lakshmana soothes Rama's agitation, be it anger or grief, we can still argue that he is verbalizing and articulating the other side of Rama, the one where Rama is instinctively 'gentle and compassionate and devoted to the welfare of all creatures'.

Rama and Lakshmana's closeness, their dependence on each other, is never in doubt. After Sita has been abducted, Rama expresses his deep and abiding love for his brother on many

---

[6] Sattar, *Valmiki's Ramayana*, chap. 34.

occasions. When Lakshmana is felled by Indrajit's snake arrows on the battlefield, Rama breaks down and weeps.

> 'What use to me is Sita or my life when I see my brother lifeless like this on the battlefield? If I looked hard enough, I would find another woman like Sita in this world. But I would never find anyone like my brother Lakshmana, my companion and adviser! If Lakshmana dies, I will kill myself in front of all the monkeys! ... Damn me and my ignoble acts that have led to Lakshmana lying like this, covered with arrows, as if he were dead! Ah Lakshmana! You always comforted me and cheered me! Now I am filled with sorrow and you say not a word! I shall follow this brave hero to the world of the dead just as he followed me into the forest!'[7]

With an intimacy such as this, it would not be surprising for the brothers to share thoughts, to bring out the best in each other, to remind one another when they are doing wrong, to reinforce each other's decisions and actions as needed.

We are accustomed to the idea that Lakshmana defers to Rama in all matters of importance, that he follows his brother's decisions without question. But even a casual reading of the Valmiki Ramayana will show us that Lakshmana differs from – rather than defers to – his elder brother more often

---

7 Sattar, *Valmiki's Ramayana*, chap. 59.

than we would imagine. Typically, it is Rama's notions and understanding of dharma that Lakshmana challenges.[8]

The first and most dramatic instance of such a challenge to Rama is in the Ayodhya Kanda, when Lakshmana receives the news of Rama's exile. His immediate reaction is to imprison his father, the king, who, Lakshmana claims, has surely lost his mind. He gives vent to his anger in Kaushalya's chambers and says:

> 'How can someone who treads the path of dharma reject a son without reason, that, too, a son who is so godlike, so upright and so restrained? Which son would honour the word of a father who is so patently in his second childhood? Rama, seize the kingdom with my help before the news of the king's change of heart spreads! When I am by your side, protecting you with my bow, there is no one, not even death, who can get the better of you!'[9]

Rama calms his impetuous brother and speaks of dharma as the most important thing in the world and of how a father's wishes must be obeyed as no father would harm his child. Then, he talks about destiny, saying:

---

[8] Whatever he might be thinking and saying in terms of his own ideas of dharma, Lakshmana almost always submits to Rama's ideas of what is right. By doing so, Lakshmana lives his life, for the most part, embodying and exemplifying the dharma of a younger brother.

[9] Sattar, *Valmiki's Ramayana*, chap. 16.

> 'That which is unthinkable and which cannot be countered by any creature is an act of destiny. This is what I have learned from what has just transpired between Kaikeyi and me. Where is the man who can fight against fate which is manifest only in its workings? Joy and sorrow, fear and anger, gain and loss, existence and non-existence – destiny reveals itself in all these things. I have no regrets about the cancelled consecration and neither should you. Lakshmana, do not think badly of our mother who has taken the kingdom away from me. Understand that she was fated to do this and recognize the power of fate!'[10]

Lakshmana's response is surprising and sets up a conversation about dharma that the brothers will continue through the entire story. Arguing against fate, Lakshmana says:

> 'How can a man like you, who stands so strong and proud in the dharma of the kshatriya, sing praises of this thing called destiny? Fate is the refuge of the weak and the impotent ... I feel only contempt for a dharma that makes even someone as resolute as you vacillate like this! It is your attachment to dharma that confuses you!
>
> 'I cannot accept that all this happened because of fate. An explanation like that is for cowards, not for the brave! No capable man would ever be oppressed by the workings of destiny. And a real man would never allow fate to frustrate his aims. I will show you which is stronger, fate

[10] Sattar, *Valmiki's Ramayana*, chap. 16.

> or manliness. The people will see that fate, which reversed your consecration, has been defeated by my courage.
>
> 'My courage will turn back this fate which comes rushing headlong at us, like a rogue elephant that has broken his bonds and ignores its goad.'[11]

Lakshmana's argument against fate is simple enough – for him, a heroic kshatriya cannot surrender to an unpleasant situation by saying that it was inevitable because of fate or destiny. He objects to the determinism that fate implies, that in the face of fate the individual has no choice, unlike in the case of dharma, where a person can choose what path to take. Rama has already chided Lakshmana for wanting to overturn their father's decree and take over the kingdom in Rama's name. He has said to Lakshmana, 'Dharma is the most important thing in the world, truth is established because of it ... Give up your ignoble ideas inspired by the duties of a kshatriya! Follow my example. Take refuge in dharma and not in violence.'[12] Rama cites the kshatriya code as the root of Lakshmana's misunderstanding of what dharma really is.

But Lakshmana's argument against the dharma that Rama has chosen to acknowledge is more complicated. Lakshmana seems to be telling Rama that a dharma that supports injustice is no dharma at all. To Lakshmana, Dasharatha's coerced decree that rescinds Rama's succession to the throne is unjust for many reasons, not least because Rama is the eldest son, and therefore,

---

11 Sattar, *Valmiki's Ramayana*, chap. 16.

12 Sattar, *Valmiki's Ramayana*, chap. 16.

should be king by primogeniture.[13] For him, therefore, Rama should not be a dutiful son and unquestioningly obey his father if his obedience perpetuates an injustice.

If Rama believes in what is right, Lakshmana believes in what is just. Since dharma is multivalent and contains the idea of justice within it (especially in its public manifestation), both Rama and Lakshmana are correct in their understanding of dharma, what it springs from and what it upholds. The brothers will continue to debate their divergent interpretations of what should determine individual behaviour through their time in the forest and even on the battlefield. Lakshmana's idea of dharma as rooted primarily in justice appears to revolve around the hope that justice will be accomplished by actions that can and should address what is wrong or unfair. Dharma as righteousness, as upheld by Rama, can be about intentions only, whereas a commitment to justice means that the individual is called upon to act. Righteousness is a quality or a virtue that can exist in a person or an event, but the path of justice requires an intervention. Thus, Lakshmana can argue against capitulating

---

[13] When Lakshmana sees Bharata approaching Nandigrama with his army and his royal entourage, his first reaction is attack Bharata who has surely come there for no good reason. He says, 'I want to see Bharata who has brought this terrible calamity upon us! Rama, he has deprived you of the kingdom and kingship. Now that your enemy has arrived here, I shall kill him! There is nothing wrong with killing Bharata, Rama! To kill someone who has harmed you is not a violation of dharma.' (Sattar, *Valmiki's Ramayana*, chap. 25) It might appear that Lakshmana is being impulsive, but in fact, he has a reason for wanting to kill Bharata. It is the same reason as he had for wanting to imprison Dasharatha, which is that it is Rama who must be king in Ayodhya.

to fate or destiny, which he sees as being fundamentally against action. Such a submission is a passive resignation to let things be as they are, even if they are wrong. One might even say that Lakshmana is driven more by the idea of a 'greater good' than Rama, whose actions stem, essentially, from his personal circumstances and situation and an insistence on his own conduct being considered unimpeachable.

For all the stoicism that Rama displays when he is told about his banishment, he is troubled by his father's actions and the dharma that allowed him to act the way he did. On their first night away from the city, Rama says to Lakshmana, 'When I think of the disaster that has befallen me as a result of the king's infatuation I feel the pursuit of pleasure must be even more compelling than the pursuit of wealth or dharma.'[14] Here, Rama is referring to the purusharthas, the so-called 'goals of human life', which are stated to be artha (wealth/power), kama (desire/pleasure), dharma and moksha (release from the cycle of rebirth) and correspond, roughly, to the various phases in a man's life. Rama despairs of the fact that Dasharatha has chosen kama (his love for his wife Kaikeyi) at a time in his life when he should, more appropriately, be interested in dharma, that is, thinking upon the basis for ethical behaviour. It is noteworthy that in Rama's distress, when he compares the importance of dharma to that of the other purusharthas, he is placing dharma within a hierarchy of values, thus acknowledging that human life can have other legitimate and sanctioned goals. Dharma, however, remains the highest pursuit of them all.

---

[14] Sattar, *Valmiki's Ramayana*, chap. 21.

Rama further says, 'He who abandons wealth and dharma and chases after pleasure shall soon destroy himself, like Dasharatha did!'[15] As he concludes his lament, Rama says, 'I could easily conquer Ayodhya and the entire earth in anger with just my arrows. But one should never use one's strength without reason. If I do not crown myself today, Lakshmana, it is only because I fear the consequences of violating dharma in my next life!'[16] This statement seems to imply that dharma is the ultimate value for Rama, outside of the other legitimate goals that a man might pursue. While Rama seems to be concerned about acting in and upholding dharma itself, Lakshmana pursues an answer to what constitutes dharma, as we have seen from his criticism of Dasharatha's behaviour.

Lakshmana's arguments with Rama are never more forceful and persuasive than when they are in the thick of the war with the rakshasas. Indrajit has just created a phantom Sita, and holding her in his chariot high in the sky above the battlefield, he slashes her across her body and 'kills' her in full view of the monkey army. When he hears what has happened, Rama collapses in a paroxysm of grief, unable to fight any longer. Lakshmana consoles him as best he can and then, somewhat unexpectedly (given the place and time), launches into an attack on the dharma in which Rama seeks refuge, the dharma Rama claims as the basis of all his actions.

> 'All this talk of dharma is futile!' he said. 'Your adherence to dharma has not protected you from all these calamities. We

[15] Sattar, *Valmiki's Ramayana*, chap. 21.

[16] Sattar, *Valmiki's Ramayana*, chap. 21.

cannot see dharma the way we can see other objects. I am beginning to believe that there is no such thing! If dharma really did exist, Ravana would be in hell and you would not be suffering like this! Ravana suffers nothing. Has dharma become adharma? If dharma did exist, nothing bad should ever happen to you!

'Or maybe dharma rallies around might, it supports the strong. Which means that we should never ally ourselves with the weak. If dharma helps only the mighty, then give up your allegiance to it and rely, instead, on your strength. Taking refuge in either dharma or adharma on principle is ultimately destructive. A man should choose which of them to follow according to circumstances.

'You cut at the root of dharma when you renounced the kingdom. Purposeful action flows from the accumulation of wealth from all possible sources, like rivers from a mountain. Men who lack wealth and power can never act in any significant way. The man who renounces wealth will continue to hanker after pleasure because he is accustomed to it. That will lead him to unethical practices … I do not know what you were thinking about when you gave up the kingdom!

'Wealth gives access to pleasures and happiness, to the fulfilment of desires. It sustains a man's pride and allows him to cling to dharma. You were obedient to your father's wishes and went into exile. A rakshasa abducted your wife who is dearer to you than your own life. As a consequence of all that, Indrajit has brought this disaster upon you today.

> 'But I shall put and end to all this! I shall release my anger and avenge the killing of Sita. I shall raze Lanka to the ground, along with all its elephants and chariots! I shall kill the king of the rakshasas!'[17]

Always ready to act, Lakshmana repeats what he had said to Rama in Ayodhya, when they learned of Dasharatha's decree. On that occasion, Lakshmana had been angry with Rama for surrendering to what he called fate – Lakshmana declared that a man's will was far stronger than anything fate could throw at him. Here, too, he is berating Rama for feeling helpless, for ascribing his situation to misfortune and fate when he could act to challenge it, if not actually change it.

At this late juncture in the story, Lakshmana appears to echo the brahmin Jabali who was present when Bharata came to Rama in Nandigrama, begging him to take back the kingdom. Jabali sounds like a materialist philosopher, either from the Charvaka or the Lokayata schools. In that sombre gathering that considers the dharma of a king and debates whether or not Rama is entitled to take the kingdom back now that his father has died, Jabali speaks with great force and clarity. He says:

> 'Rama, a noble and intelligent man like you should not think like a common person! Every man is born alone and dies alone. Who is related to whom? What is the meaning of family? ... Do not renounce your father's kingdom and take the difficult path which will cause you much hardship.

---

17 Sattar, *Valmiki's Ramayana,* chap. 63.

> Crown yourself in the prosperous city of Ayodhya which waits for you like a virgin bride, her hair in a single braid! Enjoy the royal pleasure of your city as Indra enjoys heaven. Dasharatha is nothing to you and you are no one to him. You and the king are entirely unrelated to each other. The king has gone where he had to go, for that is the destiny of all mortals. You should not concern yourself with irrelevant matters!
>
> 'I feel sorry for those people who pursue wealth and those that pursue dharma. They suffer in this life and the next. See how men waste food by performing rituals for the dead! Can a dead man eat? The books that tell you to perform sacrifices, do penance and give gifts are written by wily men who want to help others spend their money! You are wise enough to know that there is no world other than this one. Believe in what you can see and turn your back on the unseen! Take the kingdom, as Bharata has asked you to!'[18]

Jabali strikes at dharma twice: once by saying that the rituals and prescribed practices which uphold dharma are created by charlatans and are, therefore, useless. His second strike is actually the more deadly one – by saying that families are nothing and that relationships are circumstantial, Jabali cuts at the very root of the idea that an individual's dharma is lodged in the duties that devolve from family ties and social positions. Rama does not need to follow his dharma as a son because the

---

[18] Sattar, *Valmiki's Ramayana*, chap. 26.

idea of 'father' itself has no meaning. And then, as if to seal the matter, Jabali says that there is no reality other than what we can perceive with our senses, and therefore, there can be no pretence of acting in the world for benefits in an afterlife.[19]

Lakshmana's overwrought speech to Rama during the war contains many of the same ideas – he thinks that, since dharma

---

[19] In a passage that lies outside the main text of the Baroda Critical Edition of the Valmiki text, Rama is forceful in his rejection of Jabali's arguments against dharma. Rama says that he cannot understand why his father maintained such atheists as Jabali at his court, that Jabali is a Charvaka, lacking in virtue and rejecting the beliefs of brahmins and good men. Jabali quickly retreats from the arguments that he has made thus far with so much conviction and says that he had taken on the disguise of an atheist in order to persuade Rama to return to Ayodhya. As the next sarga of the Critical Edition opens, we find Vasishtha uttering soothing words, reassuring Rama that Jabali did, in fact, know the truth and had spoken in this contrary manner only to take Rama back to the throne that was truly his. Even though the Critical Edition does not include Rama's reprimand of Jabali, the fact that the next sarga opens with Vasishtha explaining that Jabali was not, in fact, a non-believer in the Vedas, shows that the larger text acknowledges Jabali recanting his words. Either way, it is clear that the Valmiki text wanted what might have been the so-called Charvaka arguments to be included in this episode, perhaps simply to let readers know that the idea of dharma was contested even as it was being defined. For details and a fuller translation, see p. 391, *The Ramayana of Valmiki, vol. 1*, translated by Hari Prasad Shastri (London: Shanti Sadan, 1957) and pp. 358–361, *The Rāmāyanā of Vālmīki: An Epic of Ancient India, vol. 6: Yuddhakānda*, edited and translated by Robert P. Goldman, Sally J. Sutherland Goldman, and Barend A. van Nooten (Princeton: Princeton University Press, 2009).

cannot be 'seen' (perhaps he means since it is not empirically demonstrable and remains relative and contingent at all times), it may not exist. He also has scant respect for Rama upholding Dasharatha's wishes simply because he was their father. But while Jabali rejects the pursuit of wealth, Lakshmana believes that it is wealth that allows a man to be dutiful and fulfil his obligations. At the height of his frustration with Rama, Lakshmana even says that a man who wishes to be effective in the world should choose dharma or adharma according to the situation.

Lakshmana's disenchantment with the idea of dharma appears to develop over the course of his experiences. At its most compelling, Lakshmana's argument for a dharma which differs from that of his brother is that justice rather than righteousness should be the basis for good and for 'correct' action, that one might even choose a so-called adharma if it were to support justice. This is most clearly visible when Dasharatha announces that Rama has to spend fourteen years in exile in the forest, and Lakshmana thinks it is not only appropriate to disobey the old king but that it is acceptable to place him under arrest for violating dharma. Justice is also the basis for his anger against Sugriva who seems to have forgotten his part of the bargain with Rama – that after being installed as king of the monkeys in Kishkindha with Rama's aid, he would begin the search for Sita.

Nonetheless, the shift, however gradual, from a search for the basis of dharma to a complete rejection of it, is radical. After Ravana has been killed and the war is over, Lakshmana watches Rama's public censure of Sita with great discomfort. He is unable to meet Sita's eyes when she asks him to make a fire for her to enter so that she can prove her innocence. One might imagine that, yet again, Lakshmana is wondering about a dharma that has no place for justice within itself, or a dharma that does not set justice as its highest goal.

After the return to Ayodhya and Rama's coronation, Lakshmana and his other brothers become Rama's lieutenants and advisers. When Rama decides that Sita must be banished because of the citizens' gossip, he turns to Lakshmana, once more, to do what he himself cannot. Lakshmana must take Sita to the forest on the pretext of visiting the sages' wives whom she had befriended earlier. He must leave Sita in the forest, far from her friends but close to Valmiki's hermitage. Again, Lakshmana wordlessly obeys his brother's wishes but the turmoil in his heart is apparent from his tears as he drives Sita away from the city.

> When they reached the further shore of the Ganga, Lakshmana joined his palms and in a voice choked with tears, he said to Sita, 'My heart is filled with grief when I think of how the world will condemn me for this, but I am acting on the orders of a wise and noble man. I would prefer death to what I have to do today, this thing which will bring me disgrace in the world! Forgive me! Do not hold this against me, good lady!' cried Lakshmana and sank to the ground.[20]

Although Lakshmana assures Sita that she will be safe in Valmiki's hermitage, it is hard for him to leave her alone on the riverbank as evening falls.

---

[20] Sattar, *Valmiki's Ramayana*, chap. 69.

> Lakshmana was too upset to speak and he kept his eyes fixed on the ground. Weeping aloud, he honoured Sita and climbed back into the boat. When he reached the other shore, he quickly got into the chariot, unable to bear the burden of his grief. He kept turning around to look at Sita as she stood there, alone and vulnerable, but he had to go onwards.[21]

It could be that Lakshmana simply cannot fathom a dharma that requires a beloved wife to be expelled from the kingdom for no fault of her own. But here too, Lakshmana's silence about dharma is intriguing, especially since Sita addresses dharma directly in the message she sends her husband through his brother.[22] She says:

> 'Do as you were told, Lakshmana! Abandon me, a poor, wretched woman! You must obey the king. But listen to what I have to say. Bow to all my mothers-in-law and touch their feet. Give them my greetings. Give them and the king my best wishes for their welfare. Tell the king, "Always treat your subjects as you would your own brothers. That

---

21 Sattar, *Valmiki's Ramayana*, chap. 69.

22 Here, as with Rama's heartless rejection of Sita after the war, Lakshmana's silence, despite his discomfort, recalls the silence of Bhishma and the other elders in the Mahabharata, when Draupadi is dragged into the Kaurava court in her stained garment after she has been staked and lost in the game of dice by her husband Yudhishthira. When Bhishma is confronted by Draupadi about what dharma would dictate in this ghastly situation, he is only able to offer her the platitude that dharma is subtle, or elusive (sukshma).

> is the highest dharma and it will earn you incomparable fame and glory.'"[23]

After Sita's banishment, the Uttara Kanda has two other crises for Rama, the king. The first is when a brahmin's young son dies for no reason. The father laments that this can only have happened if there is something fundamentally amiss in the kingdom. The sage Narada, who happens to be visiting Rama's court at the time, persuades Rama that he needs to find out where this violation of dharma, which has caused the disruption in the natural order of things, is located and that he needs to eliminate it at once. Rama kills the low-caste Shambuka who is disturbing the cosmic order by practising austerities that are not meant for him, and by doing so, brings the brahmin's son back to life. Rama acts as a king should, swiftly and without equivocation, eliminating the person whose actions threaten the well-being of his people.[24] The second crisis that Rama faces is a more personal one and occurs when he recognizes his sons at the great sacrifice he is conducting. He calls for Sita and asks her

---

[23] Sattar, *Valmiki's Ramayana*, chap. 69.

[24] The idea that the king is responsible for getting rid of anything that harms his people is displayed at the very start of Sophocles's *Oedipus the King* when a priest petitions Oedipus to attend to whatever it is that has blighted the city of Thebes. Creon returns from Apollo's shrine with a message that the 'pollution' which is causing discomfort and disease in the city has to be eliminated by banishment. As it turns out, the source of the pollution is Oedipus himself – he has killed his father and has taken his own mother as a wife. The tragedy of Oedipus unfolds from here onwards.

to prove her innocence again, in front of all his people so that they would never cast aspersions on her character again. Sita responds by disappearing into the earth, never to return. Rama is distraught, but there is nothing that he can do to bring his wife back. We are not told what Lakshmana was thinking or doing in either of these instances which are clearly moments where Rama chooses his dharma as a king over any other choices that he might have made. In fact, Lakshmana's silence about dharma in the Uttara Kanda is most unusual, given that he is deeply troubled by it in the middle books of the Valmiki Ramayana.

The Uttara Kanda accelerates after Sita's departure. Rama becomes withdrawn and quickly settles his nephews (the sons of Lakshmana, Bharata and Shatrughna) in kingdoms of their own, perhaps to protect the legacy and inheritance of his own sons who have only recently been given to him. One day, Time, in the guise of an ascetic, comes to visit Rama with a message from Brahma. Rama welcomes him.

> 'Give me the message from the sage who has sent you!' said Rama.
>
> 'I can only tell you what he said where no one else can see or hear us,' said the ascetic. 'If you care for the message the sage has sent you, then whoever sees or hears us must be put to death, Rama!'
>
> 'Send away the doorkeeper and stand there in his place,' said Rama to Lakshmana. 'I shall have to kill anyone who sees or hears our private conversation!'[25]

---

[25] Sattar, *Valmiki's Ramayana*, chap. 71.

Lakshmana stands guard at the door, and a little while later, the sage Durvasas arrives. He, too, wishes to see Rama and will not be dissuaded. He says to Lakshmana:

> 'Go at once and tell Rama that I am here! Or I shall curse you, Rama, the city and the entire kingdom as well as Bharata and all your children! I cannot control my anger!'
>
> Lakshmana considered the matter and said to himself, 'It is better that one man, I, myself, die, than all creatures be destroyed!' He made up his mind and went in to see Rama.[26]

Rama is happy to be of service to Durvasas.

> Rama was very happy until he remembered Time's words. He recalled their frightful implications and burning with grief, he hung his head and did not say a word. 'This cannot be true!' he thought to himself.
>
> Lakshmana noticed that Rama was depressed and dull, like an eclipsed moon. 'Do not grieve for me, Rama,' he said gently. 'Do as Time said, for it has been ordained. Kill me without any hesitation and fulfil your promise. The

[26] Sattar, *Valmiki's Ramayana*, chap. 71. Given what we know of how Lakshmana has been constructed by the larger Ramayana tradition, it would be easy to read this decision as Lakshmana's instinct to protect Rama's reputation. But if we follow this more conventional reading of Lakshmana's character we place him, yet again, in the shadow of his more illustrious brother and we deny him impulses and motivations that arise from his own strongly held beliefs.

man who breaks his word goes to hell! If you love me and want to make me happy, then kill me without any second thoughts or misgivings! You must nourish dharma, Rama!'

Rama's senses were in a whirl when he heard what Lakshmana said. He sent for his ministers and the family priest and told them what had happened. They were silent when they heard the story and then, Vasishtha said, 'Mighty one, I knew long ago that this calamity, this separation from Lakshmana, was going to happen! Time is all-powerful. You must abandon Lakshmana and keep your word. Dharma is destroyed when a man breaks his promise. And when dharma is destroyed, you can be sure that the three worlds with all their moving and unmoving creatures, with the gods and the sages, will also perish! You are responsible for protecting the three worlds. If you kill Lakshmana today, you will have established the universe firmly!'

'I must renounce you, Lakshmana, or else dharma will be violated!' said Rama when he heard Vasishtha's words which were filled with purpose and meaning. 'Whether I kill you or abandon you or am separated from you, it will all be the same to good men!'

Lakshmana's eyes filled with tears and he left hurriedly, but he did not go to his own home. He went straight to the banks of the Sarayu where he stopped the activities of his senses and ceased to exhale. When his breathing stopped, the gods, apsaras and groups of rishis rained flowers from the sky. Unseen by the others, Indra lifted Lakshmana's body and took him into heaven. Thus, Lakshmana reverted

> to his original state as one quarter of Vishnu and the gods and sages rejoiced and celebrated and honoured him.[27]

This is an absolutely extraordinary scene and end to the story of brotherly love and heroism. When Time arrives, Lakshmana, as always, is at his brother's side, ready to do whatever is required. Knowing that he will die if he enters the room where Rama is talking to Time, he does so anyway, sacrificing himself for the greater good. He tells Rama that he, the king, has to 'nourish dharma' and asks to be killed, for that has been ordained. Vasishtha, the gentlest of all the brahmins at Ayodhya's court, encourages Rama to kill his beloved brother so that dharma is indubitably established in the universe. And once again, Rama decides to uphold dharma by doing the unthinkable. But Lakshmana acts quickly to save his brother from performing a ghastly deed and slips away to die, alone, on the banks of the river.

In this last moment of his life, Lakshmana claims predestination as the reason for his death when he says it has been ordained. This is completely at odds with all that he has said so far about the conquest of fate, if a man is to live truly and fully, as is his statement that Rama must nourish dharma at any cost. While it is certainly true that the Uttara Kanda of what we call the Valmiki Ramayana was created by different hands and minds than the middle books of the Sanskrit text and within an entirely new theological universe,[28] Lakshmana's words and

[27] Sattar, *Valmiki's Ramayana*, chap. 71.

[28] For more on this, see Sattar, *Uttara: The Book of Answers*. The Uttara Kanda demands that we read the text backwards, as it were, with all of Rama's deeds now being viewed through the lens of his divinity and

his 'self-killing' remain remarkable and worthy of our attention. How has this man, who has sneered at the idea of fate, who has challenged the definition of dharma all his life, who has come to the point where he doubts the existence of dharma as a ground of ethical action, how has this man gone so quietly to what he calls an ordained death because either his brother or the king must nourish dharma?

As a start, we could see Lakshmana's statement that Rama must nourish dharma as neither a prescription nor a description of what dharma demands, but as an anguished cry – he knows that, however heavy the burden of doing the right thing may be, Rama will carry that burden, even at great cost to himself.[29] As Rama had maintained his father's reputation by honouring the promise he had made to his wife in a moment of weakness so many years earlier, now it is Lakshmana – who, at that time, had argued so vehemently for justice over any other principle – who preserves Rama's honour, his given word, by volunteering himself as a sacrifice. When he realizes that his brother does not have the strength to kill him, as he had promised to kill anyone that intruded on that meeting, Lakshmana walks away to still his breath and give up his human life.

---

with the entire text being reconstructed with an unchanging dharma as its foundation.

29 Lakshmana seems to echo Sita's message to Rama when she realizes that she has been abandoned in the forest. We cannot be sure that Sita is endorsing the dharma that makes Rama do what he does. She could also be expressing her anguish that Rama is unshakeable in upholding the dharma that he believes in.

It could simply be that Lakshmana welcomes death because he can no longer support Rama's actions, particularly those in relation to Sita – the public rejection after the war with the rakshasas, her humiliating banishment even though the gods had upheld her innocence in Lanka, the call for another proof of her chastity at Rama's great ashvamedha sacrifice. These actions are rooted in a dharma of righteous kingship[30] (increasingly defined by the brahmins who now dominate Ayodhya's court) that Lakshmana rejects, and arguably, can no longer live with and by. With a truly glorious generosity, Lakshmana allows Rama's idea of dharma to prevail in the kingdom as he himself exits the argument.

But there is still more to consider. With this unprecedented act, has Lakshmana transcended dharma and all that it asks of a man? Has he actually broken through an existence over-determined by such vectors as dharma, karma, fate, caste, life-stage to a point where he can exercise free will by choosing how to die?[31] Typically in Hindu myth and epic, choosing the moment of one's own death is a boon that the gods give to those they favour. On the

---

[30] No doubt Rama has remained troubled by Dasharatha's choice of honouring the boons he gave his wife rather than honouring the kingly dharma that the Ikshvakus have upheld for so many generations. In order to prove that he is not like his father, Rama gives up the wife whom he loves more than anything else.

[31] The best known recipient of this precious gift is Bhishma in the Mahabharata who, after being fatally wounded in battle, stays alive for another eight days on a bed of arrows so that he can discourse on dharma and kingship to the men who will rule the Kaurava kingdom after the war.

surface of this story, Lakshmana does not choose the moment of his death though he certainly chooses its manner – ceasing to breathe rather than placing the burden of fratricide on Rama. However, one can still be tempted to argue that Lakshmana knowingly and consciously chose to place himself in the path of death. I believe that he does this in two ways: first, by interrupting Rama's conversation that he knew carried the penalty of death, and second, by deflecting Durvasas's curse away from Ayodhya and its people.

If the Ramayana were a modern novel, we would be asking the question of whether or not Lakshmana's actions constitute a suicide. But in the world of myth and epic, particularly the Hindu world of myth and epic, the individual is a relational being and a determined being: determined by the prospective force of her/his own actions and choices, even over many lifetimes. Suicide remains the single most powerful act of free will within this determined universe, establishing the individual's ultimate control over their own life and death without intervention from the gods or any other outside forces. By ending his life in such a manner, ironically, by doing what is right and not just, Lakshmana has thrown the ultimate challenge to his dharma-upholding brother who has always chosen the more difficult path, the path of righteousness. He has demonstrated where unmitigated righteousness can lead – for Lakshmana, it is the destruction of the self.

RAMA AND THE ASCETIC IDEAL

On more than one occasion in the Valmiki Ramayana, Rama rejects kshatriya dharma, the dharma that he was born into as a prince.[1] The first time he does this is early in the Ayodhya Kanda, when Lakshmana confronts his brother after he learns of Dasharatha's decree that will send Rama into exile. Lakshmana argues that Rama has no need to obey the command, or even the wishes, of a king who is so patently not in control of his words and deeds. He urges Rama to take over the kingdom and vows that he, Lakshmana, will stand by Rama's side as he does so. Insisting that he does need to obey his father, Rama says:

> 'Lakshmana, I know you have the greatest affection for me. I also know you are upright and restrained. Dharma is the most important thing in the world, truth is established because of it. And obeying a father's command is the highest dharma of all, as is conforming to the wishes of a mother and brahmin. I cannot disobey my father simply because Kaikeyi, our mother, asked him to command me

1 On another level of the story, this might be the dharma chosen for him when Vishnu was persuaded by the other gods to be born as a human so that Ravana could be defeated.

> thus. Give up your ignoble ideas inspired by the duties of a kshatriya! Follow my example. Take refuge in dharma and not in violence.'[2]

The second occasion is when Bharata comes to the forest to plead with Rama to take back the kingdom that was so unfairly denied him, the rightful heir to the throne of Kosala. Bharata arrives with an enormous royal entourage – the mothers, courtiers, retainers, an army, ministers and the family priest, Vasishtha. Bharata says that it is not appropriate for Rama to renounce the kingdom now that their father is dead, that it is not the right thing for a king to live in the forest like an ascetic. He says, 'How can a kshatriya live in the forest? How can a king have matted hair?'[3] Rama, however, is not to be dissuaded from the path that he has chosen to take and after a fairly long and complicated discourse on what Bharata should do to be a good king, he says:

> 'How can I fail to carry out my father's promise when I am committed to it by an oath of truth? I cannot violate my father's bond with truth out of greed, delusion or even out of ignorance! Gods and ancestors reject the offerings of men who are fickle and do not keep their word. It is clear to me that every man must hold to the truth, that it is his dharma. It is for this reason alone that ascetics command so much respect. I renounce the dharma of a kshatriya because it is fundamentally unrighteous even though it has

---

2 Sattar, *Valmiki's Ramayana*, chap. 16.

3 Sattar, *Valmiki's Ramayana*, chap. 26.

> some good things about it. It attracts the base, the cruel, the greedy and those inclined to be wicked.'[4]

Between these two declarations of his disenchantment with kshatriya dharma, Rama has debated dharma with Lakshmana and expressed anguish at the principles of public and private behaviour that allowed his father to banish him from the kingdom. He is sure that his father was more dedicated to the pursuit of pleasure than he was to sustaining truth and righteousness through his actions. Somewhere in these moments of despair, Rama must equate his father's conduct with his being a kshatriya, must feel that the code Dasharatha lives by allows him to perpetrate an act of such cruelty.[5] And so, when Rama speaks out against kshatriya dharma, he talks about that dharma itself being violent and cruel, attractive to base and wicked people.

Rama seems to see violence as intrinsic to the dharma of a kshatriya, and at the most obvious level, of course, he is right. One cannot be a warrior without knowing that, at some point, one will have to kill. But he is disturbed by the fact that a kshatriya might be instinctively attracted to violence or, at least,

---

4 Sattar, *Valmiki's Ramayana*, chap. 26. Rama goes on to state that it is only ascetics who are worthy of reverence in this world because they live by truth and non-violence (Baroda Critical Edition of the Valmiki Ramayana, Ayodhya Kanda 101.31).

5 Apropos of the difference between Rama's understanding of dharma and Lakshmana's, Rama does not ever describe his father's actions as being unjust. For more on this, see the essay 'Lakshmana Seeks the Limits' earlier in this volume.

is trained to think of it as necessary. Rama's discomfort with violence is echoed by Sita when she talks to him about how they should live in the forest. She says:

> 'Now that you are here with your brother and both of you are armed, you shall see many forest creatures. Inevitably, you will be tempted to use your arrows. Like dry fuel bursts into flame when it is near a fire, so too, a kshatriya's passions are ignited when he has a bow at hand ... A kshatriya should use his bow in the forest only to protect the oppressed. What a difference there is between the life of weapons and that of the forest, between the vows of a kshatriya and those of an ascetic! We must learn to respect the code of behaviour of the world we now inhabit. Here, the mind is perverted by extreme proximity to weapons. You can return to the code of the kshatriyas when we go back to Ayodhya!'[6]

Rama responds by promising Sita that he will use his weapons only to protect the forest-dwelling sages who have asked him to keep them safe from the rakshasas who harass them and interfere with their rituals and ceremonies.

By making this argument, Rama seems to suggest that there are times when violence is justified, that there is such a thing as righteous violence. He does not, however, state that explicitly, and it is Sita who takes this implication forward and cautions Rama against gratuitous violence, or violence that is based

---

6 Sattar, *Valmiki's Ramayana*, chap. 28.

specifically in might. She says to Rama at the same moment in the forest, that the 'weakness which men succumb to because of their passions, the inflicting of violence and cruelty upon other beings without reason or enmity, that weakness appears to be present in you now ... May it never happen that you attack the rakshasas of the forest without reason, simply because you carry a weapon. I cannot bear the thought of innocents being killed, O hero!'[7]

Rama is not the only kshatriya who is concerned about the violence that his dharma demands of him. The Mahabharata was being composed at roughly the same time as the Ramayana, and in a discussion such as this, Arjuna's dilemma in the Bhagavad Gita comes immediately to mind. It is important to note that Arjuna expresses his problem not as one in which he has to kill, but as one in which he has to kill his elders, his teachers and members of his family. In that regard, the answer that Krishna gives Arjuna is the only answer that is possible for a kshatriya to receive – it is a warrior's dharma to kill and he must perform that task with detachment and diligence.

The Mahabharata presents us with another perspective on the dilemma of righteous and/or necessary violence in the character of Yudhishthira, who is, arguably, the hero of that epic.[8] Yudhishthira was always a reluctant king, especially after

---

[7] Sattar, *Valmiki's Ramayana*, chap. 28.

[8] We could argue about who the 'hero' of the Mahabharata is, with Arjuna being Yudhishthira's primary rival for that position. But I believe that, since the Sanskrit epics are fundamentally about rightful and righteous kings, we have to take Yudhishthira, who not only becomes king but thinks about what that means, as the hero of that

the fratricidal war that placed him on his ancestral throne in Hastinapura. Before that, he was a warrior of middling prowess on the battlefield, more inclined towards conversations with sages in the forest, and persistent in his desire to understand what a king should do. Given his doubts about what is the right action, it is ironic that Yudhishthira is the embodiment of dharma[9] in the Mahabharata – he is the son of Dharma, the first of the gods Kunti called upon for the birth of a son after she was married, and he is often spoken of and addressed by

---

narrative. Also, at the end of their lives, it is Yudhishthira who is singled out for an epiphany. When Yudhishthira reaches heaven (his brothers and wife having fallen along the way during their arduous climb into the mountains), he sees his enemies, the defeated Kauravas, enjoying celestial pleasures. Aghast that they have been rewarded thus for the lives they had lived, Yudhishthira asks to be allowed to be with his brothers and wife, who have been sent to hell. As he decides to join them in their torments, Indra appears and tells him that this was his last test, the last of the illusions that would bring him closer to the truth.

9 In the Mahabharata, Dharma is also embodied in the yaksha who questions Yudhishthira at the lake in the Vana Parvan, and in the dog that follows the Pandavas in their final journey to heaven. In a loaded aside, Krishna considers Vidura – brother to Pandu and Dhritarashtra, born of Vyasa and the maid who takes the place of the young Kaurava queens who are too repulsed to sleep with the forest sage again – to be the embodiment of dharma. He calls him Dharmaraja, the lord of dharma. Vidura is effectively the prime minister to the blind Dhritarashtra after Pandu has retired to the forest. Later in the story, when Dhritarashtra, Gandhari and Kunti leave the devastated kingdom, Vidura goes with them. As he dies in Yudhishthira's arms, Vidura hands over his powers to him and tells him that he, too, is Dharmaraja.

the epithet 'Dharmaraja'. While Yudhishthira is certainly the most thoughtful and virtuous of all the Pandava brothers, being the son of Dharma does not help him see the path of righteousness any more clearly than those around him. He is, however, known for his commitment to truth. Yudhishthira tells his only lie during the war, but that is under pressure from his brothers as they seek a way to make mighty Drona vulnerable. But even that is not, strictly speaking, a lie – Bhima names an elephant Ashwatthama and kills it. He bellows for all to hear that Ashwatthama is dead. Ashwatthama is also the name of Drona's son, and Yudhishthira is told by his brothers and Krishna to confirm the news of Ashwatthama's death to Drona. Yudhishthira says, 'Ashwatthama, the elephant, is dead!' but he mumbles the words 'the elephant' so that Drona cannot hear them. Drona believes that his son has been killed because he has heard the news from Dharmaraja Yudhishthira. He lays down his arms and prepares for the death that stalks him in the person of Dhrishtadyumna.

Like Rama, Yudhishthira found the dharma he was born to uphold as a warrior and a king hard to comprehend, and therefore, hard to endorse wholeheartedly. Like Rama, he sought a dharma that transcended his caste and social obligations. We could further surmise that, also like Rama, Yudhishthira is attracted by the simple lives of the forest-dwelling sages who spend their time thinking about larger and more profound questions. It is here, when the Pandavas are in exile in the forest (as a consequence of the dice game that Yudhishthira lost), that Draupadi berates him for his lack of interest in her past humiliation and her current predicament, for his lack of commitment to the impending war, and for his disregard for kingship.

But it is after the apocalyptic war that Yudhishthira is truly appalled by what he and his brothers have wrought in their determination to reclaim their contested patrimony from the cousins they grew up with. Yudhishthira appears to be the only one of the Pandava brothers who is disturbed by the pyrrhic victory they have secured – a land laid waste, an empty treasury, a city filled with grieving women, a decimated population, and a family destroyed by ferocious killings on the battlefield. He criticizes the dharma of kshatriyas that can call for and justify such violence. Like Rama, Yudhishthira associates certain human qualities and motivations for action with the compulsions and demands of kshatriya dharma, and contrasts those with the precepts that guide the lives of the forest dwellers. In the Shanti Parvan, even as he receives from Bhishma the ethical codes by which a king should live and rule, Yudhishthira places his aching despair before anyone that he can – his brothers Arjuna, Bhima and Sahadeva, and even the great sage Vyasa:

> Yudhishthira, the soul of dharma, burned with grief. His mind was agitated and he mourned, remembering Karna, the great chariot warrior. Gripped by sadness, he sighed again and again. Then, to Arjuna, he said these words, dripping with sorrow. 'If we had wandered begging in the city of the Vrishnis and the Andhakas, our family would not have lost all their men and we would not be in this terrible situation. Our enemies have gained, the Kauravas have

got what they wanted, and we have killed our own people. What possible fruits of dharma can we obtain from that! Shame on this kshatriya behaviour, shame on our breasts filled with valour, shame on the passions that brought us to this catastrophe! Forgiveness, restraint, purity, avoiding obstacles and selfishness, non-violence and speaking the truth are to be praised – they are practised continually by those who live in the forests. Because of greed and delusion, we took to pride and arrogance. Our desire to enjoy a petty little kingdom brought us to this! Even lordship of the three worlds cannot make us happy for we have seen our family slain simply because they wanted a piece of this earth!'[10]

As their argument continues, Yudhishthira later says to Arjuna:

'You only know about weapons and about the vows in which great heroes stand. You are incapable of understanding the fundamental truths of the holy texts. Only those learned in dharma can access the subtle meanings of these texts ... No one in the three worlds knows the dharma of war as you do, and you are skilled in the performance of those various acts. But these words, replete with subtle dharma, are hard for you to understand, O winner of wealth! Don't doubt my

[10] Translated by Arshia Sattar, from the Critical Edition of the Mahabharata (Shanti Parvan 19.3–4 and 19.6–8).

> wisdom. That you know about war is certain, but you have never served the elders.'[11]

In this passage, Yudhishthira seems to suggest that, as the greatest warrior ever, Arjuna has so completely internalized the dharma of a kshatriya that he is incapable of seeing that another way of being is possible, one that renounces violence and seeks truth in a life of abnegation. As he unpacks the non-kshatriya ideals that attract him, Yudhishthira addresses Arjuna as Dhananjaya, 'winner of wealth', and then goes on to say that wealth cannot be the prime motivation for action. He says, 'You are wrong when you think that there is nothing superior to wealth.'[12]

It bears noting that both Rama and Yudhishthira see their younger brothers as being largely motivated by the necessary kshatriya ideal of the quest for 'artha', which means both wealth and power. On their first night in exile, as he criticizes his father, Rama also tells Lakshmana that artha cannot be the dominant impulse for human action.[13] Rama and Yudhishthira are clearly drawn to some code of ethics that lies outside, perhaps even transcends, their varna dharma, their duties and obligations as kshatriyas. Both of them admire the way the sages live in the forest, spending their time meditating, performing rituals and

---

[11] Translated by Arshia Sattar, from the Critical Edition of the Mahabharata (Shanti Parvan 19.3–4 and 19.6–8).

[12] Translated by Arshia Sattar, from the Critical Edition of the Mahabharata (Shanti Parvan 148).

[13] See p. 137 where Lakshmana makes the argument that 'men who lack wealth and power can never act in any significant way.'

discussing the larger questions of life. Their younger brothers, Lakshmana and Arjuna, appear to inhabit kshatriya dharma fully and without any doubts, pursuing its ideals and conforming to its codes of behaviour, drawing upon this dharma for their ethics, their moral judgements of others, and for their own actions.[14]

Rama's and Yudhishthira's attraction to the ascetic way of life can perhaps be better understood if we step back and consider what we know about the larger social and religious milieu in the fifth century BCE, when the earliest layers of the epics were being composed and compiled. We know that the major Upanishads were also being composed during this period.[15] The quietism and introversion suggested by these texts are in stark contrast to the largely external and ritualized life prescribed by the expanded Vedic corpus. Apart from introducing an entirely new vocabulary of spiritual ideas and practices, the Upanishads also suggest a shift in spiritual power. Brahmins as a class are

---

[14] This difference between the Ikshvaku brothers and the Pandava brothers could well be another narrative space in which the epics draw out the tension between priest and warrior, both entitled to seek power, as well as the tension between the ascetic and the worldly, as will be discussed further, below.

[15] Scholars believe that the earliest Upanishads, the *Brihadaranyaka* and the *Chandogya*, were probably composed around the eighth century CE and are likely to be pre-Buddhist. It is also very likely that the twenty-third Jain tirthankara, Parshvanatha, lived around this time. The period of Upanishadic composition probably extends until the start of the Christian Era. These dates, as 'accurate' as any dates for ancient Indian literature can be, would hold within themselves, largely, the period of epic composition which is regarded as 500 BCE to about 200 CE.

no longer the sole intercessors between the world of humans and the world of the gods. Further, the individual brahmin is no longer the only holder of spiritual wisdom and knowledge. Gently but firmly, the Upanishads insert kshatriya kings, such as Janaka[16] and Ajatashatru, into the mix of philosophers and teachers who are the foundation of the new paradigm that searches for a higher truth. In the *Brihadaranyaka Upanishad*, Ajatashatru bests the brahmin Balaki Gargya in a debate about the nature of the ultimate reality, proving each time that the brahmin was attached to a physical manifestation of an abstract truth. Also in the *Brihadaranyaka*, Janaka is the king who questions the brahmin Yajnavalkya so that his teacher reaches a better and higher understanding of the truth.

Around the same time (sixth to fifth century BCE), the historical Buddha is born, as is Mahavira. Both belong to ruling kshatriya families, both renounce their social and political inheritance by adopting a life and values that could not be more opposed to what is expected of a king. Historically, from what we know, as well as hagiographically, from sectarian and partisan accounts of their lives, this continues the shift that is visible in the Upanishads – the warrior/king who is interested in seeking spiritual wisdom. The lives of the Buddha and Mahavira consolidate that shift in thought and aspiration by showing us a

---

16 It is not clear whether this is the same King Janaka as Sita's father in the Ramayana, although many readers and tellers of Rama stories assume that it is the same person, depicting Sita's father, Janaka, as a wise and sage-like figure, a contemplative philosopher king who is a marked contrast to the more warlike Ikshvakus who rule over an opulent court and a wealthy kingdom.

prince who goes beyond seeking the pleasures of philosophical and spiritual discourse and is capable of a profound renunciation of worldly life. Moreover, he can become a spiritual adept and a teacher.[17]

In a wider religious atmosphere that was increasingly embracing the non-violence preached by Mahavira and Gautama Buddha, the Hindu epics kept pace by placing the discussion of violence at the centre of the warrior's/king's dilemma. The discussion around violence that is occasionally (if not always) necessary, and therefore, righteous, is appropriately located in the caste dharma of the kshatriyas. And this concern with violence is surely one of the reasons that Rama and Yudhishthira hesitate to fully embrace the kshatriya dharma of their forefathers and families. Non-violence (ahimsa) affects not only what a man does and what is done to him in this life, but also has karmic implications for the lives to come. With religious merit, spiritual advancement and liberation from the cycle of rebirth now tied to non-violence, the endorsement and performance of violence becomes part of a complex universe of moral and existential choices.

What we are seeing here is not just a new horizon in a culture's understanding of the relationship between the individual, the so-

---

[17] There is a well-known legend about a prophecy at the time of Gautama Buddha's birth. When the infant prince's horoscope was cast, the seer reading it said that the boy would grow up either to be a chakravarti (an emperor) or a spiritual leader. When Gautama renounces kingship and becomes the Buddha, the sweet irony is that he becomes a chakravartin in the true etymological sense of the word, 'a turner of the wheel (of dharma)'.

called divine (or absolute) and the world; we are also witnessing a great social upheaval, as temporal and spiritual power moves away from the priestly class. Hierarchies of caste are in flux, and it is the epics that explore and express this new dynamic.

In both the epics, there are characters who inhabit the behaviour and manners of a caste that is not theirs, specifically, brahmins who live like kshatriyas and vice versa. In the Ramayana, Vishvamitra, born a kshatriya but determined to rise to the status of a brahma-rishi, becomes Rama's martial preceptor, teaching him the use of powerful weapons. But in the rest of his life and practise, Vishvamitra imitates the brahmin sages who have devoted themselves to asceticism and the performance of prescribed rituals. Parashurama, born of a brahmin father and a kshatriya mother, also appears in the Ramayana. He is known for having eliminated the kshatriyas twenty-one times over because one of them, Arjuna Kartavirya, had killed his father. Having inflicted this merciless genocide, Parashurama then lives the life of a brahmin ascetic but remains a teacher to great warriors across time.[18] In the Mahabharata, the kshatriya prince Bhishma is the greatest warrior of them all. But he renounces his father's kingdom and takes a vow of celibacy to ensure that there are no rival heirs to his stepmother's sons. Effectively, Bhishma lives like a brahmin ascetic for his entire life. Drona, born a brahmin, becomes the most revered teacher of the martial arts and is hired by Bhishma to train his nephews, the Pandavas and the Kauravas. Drona adopts a kshatriya life so

---

[18] In the Mahabharata, Karna goes to Parashurama to master the deadly weapons that he will eventually use in the war against his unrecognized brothers, the Pandavas.

that he can take the appropriate revenge on his childhood friend, Drupada, who was of royal birth and had inherited a kingdom. Kripa, too, was a brahmin who became a great archer. But he also knew the sacred texts and was the Kaurava princes' first preceptor, even before Drona.[19]

If these stories and questions of a warrior who examines the dharma into which he was born rather than merely following it had currency during the time that the Ramayana was being composed, it is interesting to think that the epic idea of kingship might have been inflected with the notion of a man born to rule who is attracted to a life of quietude, away from the royal court and royal duties. However, unlike the real princes (Gautama and Mahavira) who are able to achieve a complete renunciation of kingship, fictional princes (such as Rama and Yudhishthira) must return to their kingdoms after a period in the forest in the company of sages and (re)claim the powers and the responsibilities of monarchy. Both Rama and Yudhishthira

---

[19] In a tragic variation of this general pattern, Karna is born a kshatriya but does not know it. He asks Parashurama to be his teacher, and one day, as his teacher lies asleep in his lap, a terrible worm bores its way into Karna's thigh. Karna braces himself against the excruciating pain because he does not want to wake Parashurama. But fate would have it otherwise, and the sage is awakened by the blood that oozes from Karna's thigh and wets his face. He demands to know why Karna did not cry out and Karna says that he did not want to disturb Parashurama. It is at that moment that Parashurama knows that Karna is a kshatriya, for no one else would have ever considered withstanding such physical agony. Enraged that he has been deceived into sharing the secrets of his most lethal weapon with a hated kshatriya, he curses Karna to forget what he has learned at the moment when he needs it most.

go into the forest because they are sent into exile, which means that they did not choose to live the ascetic life (as Gautama and Mahavira did). Rama and Yudhishthira are both attracted to the simple, contemplative life only after they have experienced it; they do not go towards it with foreknowledge and intent. But we can clearly see that neither of them resist the idea of time in the forest, away from the intrigues and power play that have developed at their respective courts. Both grew up knowing that they would be king and were trained for precisely that role. Perhaps neither thought about how contentious that elevation would be, how those around them would react, how damaging their kingship would be to family relations, and also, what principles of ethical action they would be called upon to uphold when they ascended to the throne. Yudhishthira's complete degradation at the gambling match gives him an obvious reason to step away from kingship and think about his position as the eternal rival of his Kaurava cousins as well as his position as the head of his family. Rama, on the other hand, so loved and admired by all, was deeply discomfited by the behaviour of his father and the woman whom he had always treated as a mother. For both Rama and Yudhishthira, the time in the forest is a reprieve, a chance to stop acting as others expect them to and start thinking about how their actions can be true and meaningful to themselves.

While it is clear that the Indian epics are negotiating the shift of power between warriors/kings and priests at this moment in historical time, we might also consider the fact that the epic as a genre compels the hero to leave home, to wander in parts hitherto unknown and return, eventually, as a man more suited to be king. Whether we look at Gilgamesh or the Odyssey, the Ramayana or the Mahabharata, the hero's transformative journey is an integral element of the epic narrative. Rama's return to the throne could not be more different from Yudhishthira's. His claim to the throne is not disputed, he comes in triumph, having rescued his wife, killed her abductor and restored glory to his family. Even though the happiness and fulfilment of his reign are marred by Sita's banishment in the Uttara Kanda, Rama contains his emotions and performs his royal duties with public equanimity, if not personal ease. At this time, Rama is surrounded by brahmins. Agastya dominates the gathering and tells Rama stories from the past. There are no philosophical discussions, as this is a portrait of a king in a time of peace and prosperity. We must also remember that, in the Uttara Kanda, Rama is indubitably divine and one can presume that god has no need to debate issues of dharma or what constitutes 'truth'.

Nonetheless, it would be simplistic to understand Rama's inclination away from kshatriya dharma and towards a more detached life merely as the necessary compulsions of the type of narrative in which he appears. We have seen that other powerful ideas which challenged social mores and hierarchies were being explored at the time that the Ramayana was being composed. We also know that scholars such as T.N. Madan[20] and Patrick Olivelle[21] have remarked on the figure of the

[20] *Non-Renunciation: Themes and Interpretations of Hindu Culture* (New Delhi: Oxford University Press, 2001).

[21] *Samnyāsa Upanishads: Hindu Scriptures on Asceticism and Renunciation* (New York: Oxford University Press, 1992).

renunciant developing as a counterpoint to the householder and the priest, both of whom were enmeshed in society through the performance of rituals.[22]

The renunciant seeks to transcend rituals and social bonds, but he also seeks a truth that lies beyond the dharma that dictates the duties and responsibilities of caste and station in life. We have seen that, over and over again, Rama speaks of truth as being higher even than the dharma he has been called to and, thus far, chosen to uphold. His anguish lies in the fact that he cannot seek that truth without negating, or at least challenging, the kshatriya dharma that binds him to his obligations as a son in his early life and as a king when he returns to Ayodhya. In

---

[22] Aaron Sherraden has written persuasively about the grihastha (householder) stage of an individual's life being relatively unimportant in the Valmiki Ramayana, in his essay 'Grhasthas Don't Belong in the Rāmāyana' in *Grhastha: The Householder in Ancient Indian Religious Culture*, ed. Patrick Olivelle (New York: Oxford University Press, 2019). Despite the fact that a formal period of grihastha would be mandated for all kshatriyas, the irrelevance of this ideal can be observed in the Mahabharata as well, most obviously in the case of Draupadi's polyandrous marriage to the Pandava brothers. Could one suggest that, as Rama and Yudhishthira turn away from almost everything that a kshatriya must do, they also develop a lack of interest in this prescribed stage of life? While they are clearly interested in the way ascetics and forest dwellers live, might we go further and find in these two reluctant kings a lurking fascination with the person of the renunciant, the parameters of whose life could not be more removed from and oppositional to the lives that lie before them? This suggestion becomes more appealing when we remember that the epics were being composed soon after the historical Buddha and Mahavira had embraced a total renunciation of worldly life.

the Hindu universe, Rama is remarkable because he is willing to give up his own aspirations to ensure the stability of his kingdom, and through that, to ensure the maintenance of the cosmic order.

The renunciant remains a subversive posture, a challenge to the values and ideologies of a life lived in the world. Both the Buddha and Mahavira sparked social and spiritual upheaval, and in this historical moment, as Vedic religion began its slow transformation into classical Hinduism, it needed a conservative story, one that pulled back from the brink of what was essentially a profoundly existential choice for any individual – that of opting out of society. Rama and Yudhishthira cannot take the path of the real-life princes who went in search of a personal truth; they must come back to their kingdoms and their families. Rama, therefore, fulfils his role as a hero who returns to become king in the narrative that has been constructed around him, but outside the story, he also becomes the exemplar that a society in turmoil so desperately needs.

AFTERWORD:

HANUMAN, RAMA'S MESSENGER

It is, quite simply, impossible to speak about the Ramayana in any form without taking into account its most beloved and magnificent creature, Hanuman, the monkey. Born of Vayu, the wind god, and Anjana, an apsara cursed to live as a monkey, Hanuman is his father's equal in speed and strength, courage and ingenuity. But he retains the monkey form he inherits from his mother and displays some of the characteristics (such as restlessness, mischief and garrulous chatter) that we associate with the ordinary monkeys we see in our mundane lives. Hanuman enters the Ramayana about halfway through the story, without too much fanfare. But from the moment he enters and until Rama's return to Ayodhya, there is scarcely a moment when we are not aware of his presence, eager to do Rama's bidding and doing whatever it takes to support the success of his enterprise.

When Sugriva (who has been exiled from Kishkindha by Vali and lives on Mount Rishyamuka with a few loyal companions) sees Rama and Lakshmana enter the monkey kingdom, he is afraid that his brother has sent them to kill him. He sends Hanuman[1] to find out who the strangers are and what their

[1] We are never told, neither within the formally designated Ramayanas nor in any of the more diverse and eclectic stories that make up the

purpose might be. Hanuman negotiates an alliance between Rama and Sugriva and bears witness to their vow of friendship. After Vali has been killed, Hanuman actively becomes Sugriva's counsellor, encouraging him to keep the promises he made to Rama. When all the great monkeys have been summoned, Sugriva tells Rama that his exceptional companion, Hanuman, will lead the southern expedition to find Sita, and Rama gives the monkey his signet ring as proof that he is, in fact, Rama's messenger. After a gruelling journey that lasts over a month, the monkeys, led by Angada and Hanuman, arrive at the ocean shore, where the vulture Sampati tells them that a woman resembling Sita has been carried over the water to the island of Lanka. As the monkeys discuss who has the capacity to leap over the restless waves to the island, Jambavan reminds Hanuman of his birth and his childhood – his divine father and his celestial mother, the escapade when he tried to eat the sun and was felled by Indra, the boons and powers that he received as recompense for the god's hasty action.[2] Understanding who

so-called 'Ramayana tradition', how or why Hanuman comes to be Sugriva's loyal companion. There are many back and side stories about Hanuman, but his appearance as Sugriva's aide and counsellor is never explained.

2 The Bala Kanda of the Valmiki Ramayana has a rather less engaging story of how Hanuman came to be the great monkey that he is. When Vishnu agrees to take the form of a mortal man and come to earth in order to vanquish Ravana, who is tormenting the three worlds, Brahma urges the other gods to beget children on the monkeys and bears of the forest who will help Vishnu-as-Rama in this enterprise. Along with various other monkeys, Hanuman is born of a divine father. The Uttara Kanda also tells us about Hanuman's birth, but it takes the

he can be (or, perhaps, who he really is), Hanuman swells to an enormous size and flings himself forward into the sky. He travels through the air, overcoming various obstacles along the way and finally lands safely in Lanka. After a false start of trying to find Rama's wife inside Ravana's palace, Hanuman is able to locate Sita in the ashoka grove where she is being kept prisoner. He reassures her that he is Rama's emissary and gives her the ring from her beloved. Hanuman then decides that he should go back to Rama and Sugriva with information about Lanka's fortifications, after seeing its legendary king. He attacks various installations in the city, but allows himself to be captured and taken before Ravana. As a punishment for his audacity and the damage that he has caused, the rakshasas set his tail on fire. Hanuman escapes his bonds and runs through the city, setting it alight with his burning tail. He returns, triumphant, to his companions and they rush back to Kishkindha with the good news that Sita has been located. Hanuman is valour itself in the battle with the rakshasas, fighting alone and carrying Rama on his shoulders when necessary. When Lakshmana is close to death, it is Hanuman who is dispatched to fetch the life-giving

---

story we have heard from Jambavan and expands it to explain why Hanuman was not aware of the additional super-simian powers that set him apart from his cohort: Hanuman, emboldened by all the boons he had received as a result of his fall, grew into a very mischievous young monkey and constantly teased and harassed the peaceful sages as they performed their rituals. They cursed him to forget his powers until he needed them most. Both these versions of Hanuman's birth and childhood are connected with the idea of Rama's divinity which is clearly stated in the Bala and Uttara Kandas of Valmiki's text.

herb from a distant mountain before the sun rises. And when the war is over and Sita has been recovered, Hanuman, swift as the wind, travels ahead to give Bharata the good news that Rama is on his way to reclaim the rightful kingship that he had been denied for fourteen years. At the end of the Valmiki Ramayana, Hanuman is blessed with a special boon: he shall live as long as Rama's story is told in the three worlds.

Just as we are not told how Hanuman came to be Sugriva's trusted companion, Valmiki's Ramayana does not tell us what it is that Hanuman sees in Rama that makes the monkey so immediately enthralled by the exiled prince.[3] In the opening chapters of the Kishkindha Kanda, Sugriva is both suspicious and afraid of the strangers that he sees, but he is somewhat pacified by Hanuman's reassurances. He says to Hanuman:

> 'Mighty Hanuman! Disguise yourself as an ordinary man and go and meet them! ... If they seem friendly, gain their confidence by flattering them with praises and pleasant words! Position yourself such that I can see you and then ask them why they have come to this forest armed with bows and arrows.'
>
> Hanuman leapt off the Rishyamuka mountain, fully understanding what Sugriva wanted, and landed close

---

[3] Once the Ramayana becomes a bhakti text, this overwhelming desire to participate in Rama's mission is easily explained by what is basically a theophany – Hanuman, the devotee, sees his god standing before him and recognizes him at once. He surrenders his will and agency to the divine person whom he loves, and as a result, his own person and life story are immediately transformed.

> to Rama and Lakshmana. He threw off his own form and approached them in the guise of a mendicant. He addressed them in a sweet voice, praising them, as had been planned.[4]

Hanuman tells the princes about Sugriva's unfortunate circumstances, and then he says:

> 'My name is Hanuman and I have been sent here by Sugriva who is regarded as king by many of the important monkeys. I am the son of the wind, and I am Sugriva's adviser. Honourable Sugriva wishes to make friends with you! I can take any form that I choose and I can go anywhere I want! I have come here from the Rishyamuka mountain in the form of a mendicant to carry out Sugriva's instructions!'[5]

Rama is overjoyed to hear this, because it is Sugriva he seeks. He is also very pleased with Hanuman's demeanour and is easily persuaded to meet the deposed king of the monkeys.

> Rama took Sugriva's outstretched hand and gripped it firmly. Pleased that he had made the alliance he wanted, Rama embraced Sugriva with affection. Hanuman, meanwhile, relinquished the mendicant form that he had taken on and, in his own form, gathered some wood and

---

[4] Sattar, *Valmiki's Ramayana*, chap. 35.

[5] Sattar, *Valmiki's Ramayana*, chap. 35.

> made a fire. He worshipped it with an offering of flowers and then, with a glad heart, he placed the blazing fire between Sugriva and Rama.[6]

At this point, and even months later, when Hanuman reminds the pleasure-loving Sugriva of his promise to Rama, there does not appear to be any special attraction between Rama and Hanuman. Hanuman is diligently carrying out his duties as an adviser to a king who has just been reinstated on the throne, and as part of that role, he seems to treat Rama as a powerful and honoured ally. But when the mighty monkeys gather at Sugriva's command to begin the search for Sita, it is Hanuman who is assigned a special task. Sugriva calls him aside and praises his strength, so like his father's, and commends his many talents as a negotiator.

> Rama gazed at the enterprising monkey with deep satisfaction and felt as if his ends had already been achieved. He gave Hanuman his signet ring with his name engraved upon it so that Sita would recognize him as a messenger from Rama ... The great monkey took the ring and honoured it by placing it upon his head. Then he touched Rama's feet and joined his palms and set off on his journey. At the head of the monkey army, Hanuman, son of the wind, looked like the moon surrounded by stars in a cloudless sky. 'Son of the wind, with your strength and

6 Sattar, *Valmiki's Ramayana*, chap. 35.

> courage that rivals a lion's, I depend on you to find Sita!' said Rama.[7]

This significant moment, when Rama hands over his ring and appoints Hanuman his own messenger, has to be the point at which Hanuman becomes aware of the import and gravity of the task that has been assigned to him alone. However, in the Valmiki text, this comes across as simply a moment when a trusted retainer (Hanuman), recognized by the person whose enterprise is being furthered (Rama), is elevated to a higher task and rises to the additional responsibility and status. In one way, Hanuman is extending his role as Sugriva's lieutenant by taking on the task that their new ally needs performed. But as the text's audience, we cannot fail to notice that from this point in the story Hanuman identifies himself as his father's son and as Rama's messenger before he mentions Sugriva. Naming Rama first as the person he represents in the mission to rescue Sita need not be merely an act of protocol on Hanuman's part. We might ask if Hanuman has actually found a more charismatic leader in Rama and if he has switched loyalties. If so, we should think about which of Rama's acts or deeds, thus far, have moved Hanuman such that he now finds Sugriva less adequate, less worthy of the enormous power and the many skills that he has to offer.

Hanuman has but recently witnessed Rama going against all the rules that govern a kshatriya's actions when he is fighting. Rama has agreed to kill Vali, with whom he has no enmity; he

---

[7] Sattar, *Valmiki's Ramayana*, chap. 42.

has shot Vali, who was engaged with another opponent at the time; he has shot Vali while he himself was hidden; and he has shot Vali in the back.[8] Vali has challenged Rama's adherence to the dharma that he upholds. He says:

> 'You are a prince, handsome and distinguished. You carry all the outward signs of dharma. How could someone like you, born a noble kshatriya, all of whose ethical doubts are resolved by the wise, how could you do something so cruel, hidden behind the trappings of dharma?'[9]

Rama responds by saying, in no uncertain terms, that whatever a monkey considers dharma is of no consequence.

> 'Your criticisms of me are childish and immature, for you have not truly understood the meaning of dharma, artha, kama or worldly living. You have never been exposed to the teachings or the wisdom of learned men and yet you, with your monkey nature, presume to teach me! The earth with its mountains and forests belongs to the Ikshvakus. They have the right to condemn all the birds, beasts and men who inhabit it! It is ruled by the righteous

---

[8] One of the later stories of Ramayana characters that fall outside the canon, as it were, explains Rama's caution (hiding, shooting him in the back) when he has to kill Vali for Sugriva's sake: Vali had a boon by which he absorbed half the strength of anyone who faced him in combat, thereby making himself stronger and his opponent weaker. Rama hid from Vali so that he would not fall victim to Vali's boon.

[9] Sattar, *Valmiki's Ramayana*, chap. 38.

> and honourable Bharata … We and other kings execute his orders, which are rooted in dharma, here and all over the earth, so that the eternal dharma may flourish … You have transgressed the bounds of dharma. Your conduct is inappropriate because you are ruled entirely by pleasure. You are not fit to be a king! … Monkey, the dharma followed by truly good men is subtle and hard to understand. How can a fickle creature like you, who learns from equally fickle monkeys, know anything?'[10]

Perhaps it is this enunciation of dharma that moves Hanuman, that makes him realize that the values and codes of kshatriya dharma are not absolute. And also, that there is a way to behave that extends beyond what he knows in his essential monkey nature.[11] That way of righteousness is predicated on a higher truth, and Hanuman sees that Rama seeks to act always in

---

[10] Sattar, *Valmiki's Ramayana*, chap. 38.

[11] The Sanskrit word that I am translating as '(essential) monkey nature' is kapitvam. Hanuman is profoundly aware of the limitations of this disposition, one that he shares with all the other great monkeys. When Sugriva is convinced that the armed princes he sees by the Pampa lake have been sent by Vali to kill him, Hanuman admonishes him by saying, 'Your wicked brother, whom you fear so much, is nowhere to be seen, my friend, and I see no cause for alarm! Unfortunately, you have just displayed your essential monkey nature! Your mind is so flighty and distracted that you cannot even sit in one place and consider the situation calmly.' (Sattar, *Valmiki's Ramayana*, chap. 35) Later, during his own adventures in Lanka, Hanuman continually scolds himself for succumbing to kapitvam when he panics or is distracted or is inclined to make a decision without taking into account all that he knows.

and through an understanding of it. Hanuman's acceptance of Rama's ring (albeit as a courier to the person for whom it is finally intended) could be seen as an initiation into this transcendent dharma that Rama offers.

How is it, though, that Hanuman is free to choose the dharma that he wishes to follow? If, indeed, Hanuman has chosen one dharma (the one espoused by Rama) over another (that of his fellow monkeys, who are warriors), how does he think about his own actions and his motivations? Does Hanuman, like Vibhishana, have to think about the difference between the way he acts as a monkey and the way he should act when he is compelled by the principles that guide human behaviour?[12]

Hanuman is born of parents who are unlike each other: his father is a god and his mother is a monkey who is a cursed celestial (but not divine) woman. Because of this miscegenation, we could argue that Hanuman is a liminal being, living on the borders of more strict categories of existence, each of which are, in the Hindu universe, constrained by complex rules of appropriate action. Liminality could, then, offer choices of behaviour and, perhaps therefore, even choices of dharma. With other beings that we might consider liminal on the basis of such miscegenation (such as Ravana and his siblings), the choice about which dharma they follow depends on what is presented to them as their heredity – Ravana is born demonic and reinforces his rakshasa nature with the way he chooses to

[12] The arguments about Vibhishana's svabhava and svadharma, in the essay 'The Good Monkeys and the Bad Rakshasas' earlier in this volume, could apply here as well.

live, while Vibhishana, on the other hand, seizes the chance he is offered by his birth and lives virtuously in righteousness.

Hanuman's character and his natural qualities are, loosely, a combination of kshatriya and brahmin attributes. From his father Vayu, he inherits the skills and qualities that define a warrior – his speed, agility, courage, strength, and the ability to change his shape and size.[13] Most often, Hanuman's speed and power are likened to that of the Wind and his valour and prowess in battle are unsurpassed among the monkeys. But Hanuman is also learned in the ancient texts. He is celibate, a brahmachari, a fact that is celebrated in the mainstream Ramayana tradition of the Indian subcontinent. The virtues of learning and sexual discipline are usually associated with brahmins (by both ascription and prescription). Hanuman could not have inherited a temperament inclined to scholarship and asceticism from either of his parents, and so we must look to the boons he received as an infant to locate these propensities that are also part of his makeup. In the Uttara Kanda version of Hanuman's birth story, 'The sun, the blessed one who drives away the darkness spoke. "I shall give him one-hundredth of

---

[13] In the Vedic tradition, Vayu, like Indra and others, is a warrior god, and it is no surprise that Hanuman embodies many of his father's martial aspects. The Bala Kanda tells us that all the monkeys born of the gods can change their shape. But in the version of Hanuman's birth narrated by Jambavan, we are told that his mother, Anjana, had the power to change her form. Even though she was cursed to live as a monkey, she often took on the form of a lovely young woman and wandered around on her own. It was on one such occasion that Vayu saw her and desired her.

my effulgence, and when he starts to study the sacred texts, I will give him the capacity to become a scholar."'[14] While this accounts for Hanuman's knowledge, it does not give us a reason for his celibacy, which is, in any case, not an invariant feature of his many exploits and adventures.[15] Unlike so many of the other monkeys that had embarked on the search for Sita, Hanuman has no monkey family – neither parents nor siblings, neither wives nor children.[16] In this, too, he resembles a brahmin sage who goes beyond mere sexual abstention and does not allow the emotional bonds of any family to impinge upon his ascetic and

---

14 Sattar, *Uttara: The Book of Answers*, sarga 36. .

15 In stories outside the canon, Hanuman most often has a son, usually born from a drop of his extremely potent sweat that was swallowed by a fish as he flew over the ocean to Lanka. As such stories of unexpected offspring usually go, father and son do not know or recognize each other until a glorious fight in which all is revealed and they join hands to defeat Ravana. In many South East Asian Ramayanas, however, Hanuman is sexually promiscuous and fathers many sons on many different kinds of women.

16 None of Hanuman's three parents plays any role in his life at all after his encounter with Indra. His monkey father, Kesari, is little more than a name that provides an occasional patronymic for his son. Outside the Ramayana story, Hanuman has a half-brother in Bhima, born to Kunti when she calls on Vayu to give her a son. In the Mahabharata, the two brothers meet in the forest and Hanuman, the elder one, teaches Bhima about the yugas and the nature of time. He promises to appear on the battle banner of the Pandavas as a talisman and an augury of their victory in the war against their cousins. Arjuna's banner, kapidhvaja, carries the image of a rampaging monkey.

spiritual practice. Family relations determine behaviour,[17] and in a sense, the absence of family for Hanuman in the Ramayana (and the absence of the conflicting obligations that this would, of necessity, imply) also allows him to think about his choices and actions differently.[18]

What might it be, however, about the dharma that Rama espouses after he has shot Vali that so attracts Hanuman? Although Vali criticizes Rama for violating the kshatriya code in shooting him the way he did, Rama does not respond to that censure. Instead, he talks about a dharma that has nothing to do with being a kshatriya in combat; he seems to care little for that.[19] For him, Vali must be punished because he has violated the dharma that Ayodhya's kings hold as rightful, a dharma that, increasingly, seems to be about kingship and empire.

---

[17] We have seen this in Rama's choice to be a dutiful son who obeys his father's wish that he live in the forest for fourteen years. He could have chosen to act as Ayodhya's heir apparent and fight for the throne which had just been bequeathed to him.

[18] I am grateful to Samuel Tan, my student in the University of Chicago South Asia Study Abroad Program (Fall 2019), for this insight about Hanuman being free of family obligations as he makes his choices about ethical behaviour.

[19] Even in the Ramayana, Rama himself has never been a warrior of note, unlike Arjuna, for example, who is the greatest warrior of his generation. It is true that Vishvamitra teaches Rama the secrets of powerful weapons, and it is also true that Rama wins Parashurama's bow from him, but these weapons do not define him, nor do they dominate his life. In this regard, he again resembles Yudhishthira, who was also not an accomplished warrior like his brothers.

Rama has always been troubled by what kshatriya dharma asks of those who follow it – this is evident in all his conversations about dharma, no matter if he is speaking to Lakshmana, Bharata or Vasishtha. Rama seeks a dharma that sustains itself, the three worlds and the cosmic order, a dharma rooted in some higher truth that is beyond time, place and person. Perhaps he searches so desperately for a potentially universal dharma because of his own dilemmas and conflicts.[20] Rama is unable to reconcile all that has happened as the result of individuals (including himself) simply following the dictates of the dharma that kshatriyas and kings live by. He questions what dharma would persuade a father to exile his most virtuous and beloved son, he wonders what it means for him to be a good son to his father but not to his mother, he thinks about how an exiled prince can continue to live as a kshatriya in the forest, and in the end, he is distraught that the dharma of kingship has bound him to banish his beloved wife and renounce his brother.

Adherence to a dharma rooted in truth rather than in social status and roles could have made Rama's choices very different. In Hanuman's case, it is his liminality, his lack of definition and determination, that allows him the opportunity to think about what is right less subjectively, as it were. More than any other character in the Ramayana, Hanuman is entirely free to do whatever he pleases, to become whoever he wants. Within a dharma that is postulated as transcendent and eternal, independent of what or where one is, Hanuman finds a template

---

20 For a longer discussion, see Sattar, *Lost Loves: Exploring Rama's Anguish.*

for action that can be both righteous and authentic. In what is surely the Ramayana's most magnificent moment, Hanuman learns who he is and what he can do and is immediately propelled by that self-recognition to make a great leap across the water to find Sita – a leap that is literal as well as metaphorical. It is, of course, literal, because it furthers the action of the larger story; but it is metaphorical because it transforms Hanuman into full and complete dedication to Rama.

Hanuman's leap from an intuition about Rama's infallibility to his unshakeable faith in his righteousness has a short literary span, but the journey from enthusiastic aide in Valmiki's story to perfect devotee of the larger Ramayana tradition took over a millennium in historical time. In the sixteenth century, Tulsidas's own devotion to Rama transformed Hanuman into the paradigmatic bhakta, a devotee completely immersed in his love for Vishnu-as-Rama. As Hindu theology, particularly Vaishnavism, fully embraced devotion as the most fundamental relationship between the individual and the divine, Hanuman, the monkey of Valmiki's Ramayana, became a bulwark of humility and loyal service to the beloved Lord.

Everything that Hanuman becomes and embodies in Tulsidas's *Ramcharitmanas* is foreshadowed – indeed, seeded – in the story that Valmiki's Ramayana tells. But before Hanuman becomes the perfect bhakta, the narrative (and ethical) space he occupies and expands in the story of Rama points to the possibility that the transcendent dharma Rama so desperately espouses has the possibility of being a universal dharma – not because it is for everybody, but because accepting it as a guide for behaviour can be a matter of choice for anybody.

We receive the Ramayana as a manual for how to live by dharma – the dharma of being a member of a family, of being a married person, a public figure, a private individual, a member of society, a being in the three worlds. We have also learned from the Ramayana that the essence of being truly righteous is to choose one among many possible paths to goodness (however determined those paths may be by who we are and what our past actions have been). Perhaps what Rama desired most in his life was the freedom to choose without constraint. The fact that he lived his life within the rules that bound him is what makes him the maryada purushottama: despite knowing that there was a dharma which would free him, he chose not to make it his own. Liminal Hanuman, free to choose who he wants to be, thus represents the most profound challenge to the idea of the perfect man, the man who becomes the epitome of the very boundaries that restrict him.

CROSS-EDITION REFERENCE

For Arshia Sattar's Translation of the Valmiki Ramayana

HarperCollins India (2019) and Rowman & Littlefield (2018) Editions	Penguin Classics (2000) Edition
Childhood	***Childhood***
Chapter 1	Chapter 1
Chapter 2	Chapter 2
Chapter 3	Chapter 3
Chapter 4	Chapter 4
Chapter 5	Chapter 5
Chapter 6	Chapter 6
Chapter 7	Chapter 7
Chapter 8	Chapter 8
Chapter 9	Chapter 9
Chapter 10	Chapter 10
Chapter 11	Chapter 11
Chapter 12	Chapter 12

HarperCollins India and Rowman & Littlefield Editions	Penguin Classics Edition
Ayodhya	***Ayodhyā***
Chapter 13	Chapter 1
Chapter 14	Chapter 2
Chapter 15	Chapter 3
Chapter 16	Chapter 4
Chapter 17	Chapter 5
Chapter 18	Chapter 6
Chapter 19	Chapter 7
Chapter 20	Chapter 8
Chapter 21	Chapter 9
Chapter 22	Chapter 10
Chapter 23	Chapter 11
Chapter 24	Chapter 12
Chapter 25	Chapter 13
Chapter 26	Chapter 14
Chapter 27	Chapter 15
Wilderness	***Wilderness***
Chapter 28	Chapter 1
Chapter 29	Chapter 2
Chapter 30	Chapter 3
Chapter 31	Chapter 4
Chapter 32	Chapter 5
Chapter 33	Chapter 6
Chapter 34	Chapter 7

HarperCollins India and Rowman & Littlefield Editions	Penguin Classics Edition
Kishkindha	***Kiṣkindha***
Chapter 35	Chapter 1
Chapter 36	Chapter 2
Chapter 37	Chapter 3
Chapter 38	Chapter 4
Chapter 39	Chapter 5
Chapter 40	Chapter 6
Chapter 41	Chapter 7
Chapter 42	Chapter 7 (ch. no. repeated)
Chapter 43	Chapter 8
Chapter 44	Chapter 9
Beauty	***Beauty***
Chapter 45	Chapter 1
Chapter 46	Chapter 2
Chapter 47	Chapter 3
Chapter 48	Chapter 4
Chapter 49	Chapter 5
Chapter 50	Chapter 6
Chapter 51	Chapter 7
Chapter 52	Chapter 8
Chapter 53	Chapter 9
Chapter 54	Chapter 10

HarperCollins India and Rowman & Littlefield Editions	Penguin Classics Edition
War	***War***
Chapter 55	Chapter 1
Chapter 56	Chapter 2
Chapter 57	Chapter 3
Chapter 58	Chapter 4
Chapter 59	Chapter 5
Chapter 60	Chapter 6
Chapter 61	Chapter 7
Chapter 62	Chapter 8
Chapter 63	Chapter 9
Chapter 64	Chapter 10
Chapter 65	Chapter 11
Chapter 66	Chapter 12
Chapter 67	Chapter 13
Chapter 68	Chapter 14
Epilogue	***Epilogue***
Chapter 69	Chapter 1
Chapter 70	Chapter 2
Chapter 71	Chapter 3

INDEX

ACKNOWLEDGEMENTS

I never believed writers of fiction when they said that characters suddenly took over the story and began to write themselves, that there comes a point when the writer has no control over the book. I used to think that was a useless conceit: that did not pay its dues to the rigour of thinking and plotting and rejecting, of throwing out the baby with the bathwater, the real blood, sweat and tears of writing. But something very much like that happened to me with this volume of essays.

I had intended to write about the so-called minor characters in the Ramayana, such as Dasharatha and Vibhishana. I also wanted to think about major characters, such as Ravana, Lakshmana and Hanuman, and their narrative roles. I started with Dasharatha, and because he dies in the second book of the text, I thought it would be a short and manageable chapter.

It was. But Dasharatha took himself in directions that I had certainly never intended, and once he had done that, other characters in the Ramayana started to respond to the questions and problems he had laid out. Before I knew it, this had become a book about dharma, so far from what I had set out to write that we even had to change its title.

There is another misconception about writing that this book confirmed for me, the illusion that we write in isolation from the world. That is simply not true. I know that my books are made possible by the many people that support me and keep me going – some through conversations about the book, some through offering time and space to write, some through being there in the daily (and nightly) business of life. But all of these people, near and far, offer kindness, patience and love. I am deeply grateful to them all; they will never know the many times that I have thanked them in my heart over the months in which this book was written.

My mother Nazura's house and her person is always a shelter from the storm. I am able to write there with the ease that can only come from knowing that everything is where it should be and is as it should be, that the moon will shine through my window, and that the sun will rise in the east tomorrow. Ariane Fischer and Isabelle Fischer have both given me homes away from my own to think, to write and to fail in my writing. They have kept the faith long after my own has been gone and have provided food and drink, silence, 'a room of my own' (and with a view) whose worth cannot be estimated.

Rahul Soni, so much more than my editor, has been with this book not only in the chapters that I've been sending him, but through innumerable, and often interminable, late-night conversations in which ideas and contradictions lurched and swerved between us with gay abandon. No matter how far-fetched my arguments, Rahul heard and encouraged them all, allowing me to write the book that evolved rather than the one we had talked about when we started.

At a rather critical time in my life as a writer, Udayan Mitra and Ananth Padmanabhan brought all my Ramayana books to HarperCollins India. I thank them for their confidence in my work and for the faith that niche books still have a place in the world.

My agent, Priya Doraswamy, has super powers that she uses to deal with all the intimidating and truly unlovely details that stand in the way of a writer's only job, which is writing. I am fortunate that she picked me to take care of.

Ram Madhwani and Shatrujeet Nath were indefatigable in our freewheeling discussions of dharma. I thank them for opening my mind to new possibilities, for pushing me to think more clearly, and for their patience with my stubborn insistence on 'what is right'. Anmol Tikoo has always been generous in engaging with my intellectual obsessions even when they are far from his own. He has also kept me steady when I have been unsure of my own way forward in this increasingly hostile world. R. Sivapriya still reassures me with her measured comments that, nonetheless, betray her confidence in my work. From the first word I write to the last, Wendy Doniger is always in my head and by my side. Never more than a 'faster than thought' email away, she has been and is dictionary, thesaurus, editor, comma-fairy, sounding board, keeper of good spirits, wise wit, teacher, friend. I cannot imagine writing a book without her. Over thirty-five years, she has only made my work and my self better.

For laughter and tears, for keeping alive memories of a happier and fuller time, for shared dreams and collective courage, my dear friends who might think that they do not actually help me write: Arati and Shetty, Mrugank, Nayana, Poorna, Riya, Rohan, Shai, Shunnu, Trupti and Ravi.

And as this book goes out into the world, I remember Girish Karnad and Margaret Mascarenhas with love and respect – freethinkers, indomitable fighters, fearless comrades, even in the dying of the light. I shall miss them both enormously.

ABOUT THE AUTHOR

Arshia Sattar holds a PhD in South Asian Languages and Civilizations from the University of Chicago. She teaches classical Indian literature at several institutions in India, is founder and director of the Sangam House writers' residency, and writes about books and Indian literature for a number of journals and magazines. Her *Mahabharata for Children* was awarded the Sahitya Akademi Prize for Children's Literature in 2022. Her other books include: *The Mouse Merchant: Money in Ancient India*; and *Kishkinda Tails, Pampasutra, Adventures with Hanuman, Ramayana for Children* and *Favourite Stories from Hindu Myths* for children. She has been working with the Valmiki Ramayana for thirty-five years.

ALSO BY ARSHIA SATTAR

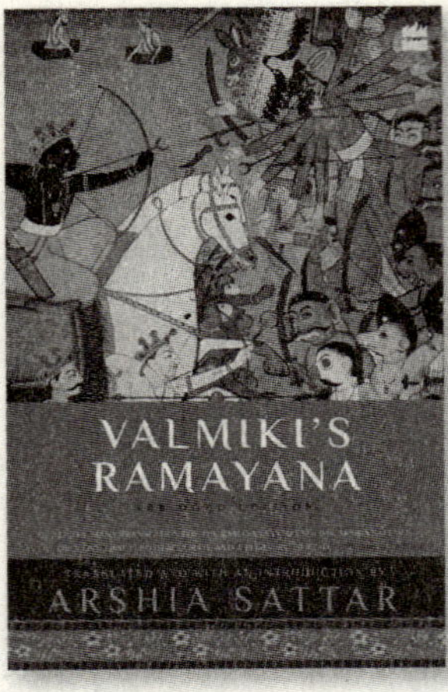

Valmiki's Ramayana

Valmiki's Ramayana, composed as early as 500 BCE, remains a story that speaks to every generation and continues to enthral millions of people in the Subcontinent and beyond. The noble prince Rama is exiled from Ayodhya on his stepmother's whim, and his loyal brother Lakshmana and beautiful wife, Sita, follow him into the forest despite the many dangers it holds. But when Sita is kidnapped by Ravana, king of the rakshasas, Rama must go deep into himself to find the physical and emotional resources he needs to rescue her. Apart from exploring the fundamental human question of how to be good, the Ramayana is also the story of a god who comes to earth to establish righteousness. The tension between Rama's essentially divine nature and his all too human trials makes this one of the most compelling epics in world literature.

Uttara: The Book of Answers

Instead of being a tranquil denouement to a tale studded with dangerous adventure and emotional turbulence, Valmiki's Uttara Kanda is a shattering epilogue to a beloved story. Ravana has been defeated, and Rama and Sita have returned to Ayodhya. Rama is established on the throne that is rightfully his and spends his time listening to the stories that the sages tell him, which answer questions like: Why did Hanuman not know about his special powers? How is it that the mighty rakshasas were defeated by the monkeys? Why did Ravana never touch Sita when she was his prisoner? But these stories are punctuated by events such as the banishment of Sita and the killing of Shambuka. What is said and done in the Uttara Kanda forces us to reconsider the events of the Ramayana, urging us to read the epic through a new and disturbing lens.

ALSO BY ARSHIA SATTAR

Lost Loves: Exploring Rama's Anguish

Below the surface of the heroic narrative of kings and warriors and the triumph of good over evil, the heart of the Ramayana beats with the tender love story of Rama and Sita. Rama and Sita's love blossoms and grows during their years in the forest, as they learn more about each other and themselves. But the challenges they face in exile, both physical and emotional, take their toll, and by the time they return to Ayodhya, a shadow has been cast upon their love. The consequences are cataclysmic. Through these remarkable essays, we see Rama and Sita at their most human and their most vulnerable—as they face the pain of separation, the darkness of misunderstanding and suspicion, and tragic loss—and, therefore, at their most accessible as exemplars of the culture they have come to define.

Tales from the Kathasaritsagara

The *Kathasaritsagara* is truly an ocean that carries the reader on its gentle swell to shores far and near, to places known and imagined, to people familiar and strange. Drawing from earlier collections of tales, the *Kathasaritsagara* was composed in Sanskrit by Somadeva in eleventh-century Kashmir. In a period and a language still largely dominated by religious texts, the *Kathasaritsagara* is a breath of fresh air. No set of beliefs dominates, no sacred texts are glorified—what it revels in most is the pulsating carnival of human life and experience. Priests and monks, gamblers and courtesans, kings and bandits, merchants and housewives, talking animals, divine and demonic beings—all cavort through its pages, in cities and forests, across seas and on islands. And in Arshia Sattar's masterful translation, the many universes of adventure the *Kathasaritsagara* holds within itself come alive for a new generation of readers.

HarperCollins *Publishers* India

At HarperCollins India, we believe in telling the best stories and finding the widest readership for our books in every format possible. We started publishing in 1992; a great deal has changed since then, but what has remained constant is the passion with which our authors write their books, the love with which readers receive them, and the sheer joy and excitement that we as publishers feel in being a part of the publishing process.

Over the years, we've had the pleasure of publishing some of the finest writing from the subcontinent and around the world, including several award-winning titles and some of the biggest bestsellers in India's publishing history. But nothing has meant more to us than the fact that millions of people have read the books we published, and that somewhere, a book of ours might have made a difference.

As we look to the future, we go back to that one word—a word which has been a driving force for us all these years.

Read.

Harper Collins · 4th · HARPER PERENNIAL · HARPER BUSINESS · HARPER BLACK · हार्पर हिन्दी

HarperCollins *Children'sBooks* · HARPER DESIGN · HARPER VANTAGE · Harper Sport